Carroll D. Wright

A Report on the total Cost and Labor Cost of Transformation in the Production of certain Articles

In the United States, Great Britain, and Belgium

Carroll D. Wright

A Report on the total Cost and Labor Cost of Transformation in the Production of certain Articles
In the United States, Great Britain, and Belgium

ISBN/EAN: 9783337154257

Printed in Europe, USA, Canada, Australia, Japan

Cover: Foto ©ninafisch / pixelio.de

More available books at **www.hansebooks.com**

55TH CONGRESS, 3d Session. } SENATE. { DOCUMENT No. 20.

A REPORT

ON THE

TOTAL COST AND LABOR COST OF TRANSFORMATION IN THE PRODUCTION OF CERTAIN ARTICLES IN THE UNITED STATES, GREAT BRITAIN, AND BELGIUM.

MADE IN COMPLIANCE WITH THE RESOLUTION OF THE UNITED STATES SENATE OF JUNE 26, 1897,

BY

CARROLL D. WRIGHT,
COMMISSIONER OF LABOR.

DECEMBER 7, 1898.—Referred to the Committee on Education and Labor and ordered to be printed.

WASHINGTON:
GOVERNMENT PRINTING OFFICE.
1899.

COST OF PRODUCTION OF CERTAIN ARTICLES.

DEPARTMENT OF LABOR,
Washington, D. C., December 7, 1898.

SIR: I have the honor to submit herewith a report upon the total cost and labor cost of producing certain articles in the leading branches of industry in the United States, Great Britain, and Belgium.

This report has been prepared in compliance with the following resolution of the Senate:

IN THE SENATE OF THE UNITED STATES.
June 26, 1897.

Resolved, That the Commissioner of Labor be, and is hereby, directed to collect from official sources, or otherwise if necessary, information relating to total cost and labor cost of production in fifteen of the leading industries common to this country, Great Britain, France, Belgium, and Germany and report the results of his inquiries to the Senate as soon after the meeting of the second session of the Fifty-fifth Congress as possible: *Provided,* That the inquiries hereby authorized shall be carried on under the regular appropriations made for the Department of Labor.

WM. R. COX, *Secretary.*

Examination having shown that the information called for by this resolution could not be obtained from official reports, it became necessary to secure it directly from the manufacturers, and experts from the Department were therefore detailed for this purpose. The provision that the investigation should be carried on under the regular appropriations for the Department has necessarily limited the scope of the inquiry to some extent. The great expense and difficulty of finding manufacturers in foreign countries able and willing to give the information sought thus made it necessary to restrict the investigation as regards European data to the two countries of Great Britain and Belgium. These two countries, however, are thoroughly representative as showing Old World conditions, and the information obtained in regard to the cost of production there, taken in connection with the data for the United States, it is believed, furnishes material substantially corresponding to that called for by the resolution.

This material is presented in the form of 446 separate statements of the cost of producing certain articles representative of the products of the great industries of agricultural implements, boots and shoes, brick, men's clothing, cotton goods, cutlery, furniture, glass, men's hats, iron and steel, leather, pottery products, and woolen goods. In the selection of the units for investigation, the effort was made to make a choice of those which were as simple in construction as possible, both because it is practically impossible to secure accurate information concerning more complicated articles, and because, if obtained, in but rare instances could the products of different establishments or countries be compared.

In making use of the information here presented it is important to understand the exact significance of the terms "cost of production" and "labor cost of production" as here employed, as both are expressions which are often used to relate to quite different statements of facts. In the present report by total cost, or cost of production, is meant the total expenditure necessary for the production of the articles considered, or, in other words, that amount at which, if the articles were sold, neither a profit nor loss to the manufacturer would result. By cost of labor is meant that part of this total amount which is expended directly for labor in the establishments making the articles considered in transforming the materials into the finished products. It thus does not include the labor expended in the previous production of these materials.

An examination of the data furnished by different establishments in the United States, as well as in Great Britain and Belgium, occasionally shows striking and apparently inexplicable differences in the labor costs and total cost of producing articles appearing from their description to be substantially alike. In some cases the divergence is such as to suggest that inaccurate figures were given by the manufacturers. This, however, is not believed to be the case. Differences as great as those shown in this report undoubtedly exist both in the total cost of producing the articles considered, and particularly in respect to the relative proportion going for labor.

Theoretically, the establishments producing the cheapest will drive other establishments out of the business. Practically, however, this is true only as a general statement, and mills producing at widely different costs are found in operation in almost all industries. Moreover, when not merely the whole product of establishments, but particular articles are considered, it is evident that the possibilities for these differences in costs become still greater. There is a great difference in various establishments in respect both to their equipment and the efficiency with which they are managed. One establishment may be completely supplied with the latest improved labor-saving machinery and be so arranged as to secure the handling of materials and their conversion into finished products with the least possible expenditure for labor, while another establishment producing the same line of goods may use old machinery, and its efficiency as regards its ability to produce cheaply be far inferior to that of the former.

Again, the general expenses may be much greater in one establishment than in another, owing to lax management, the employment of a large number of administrative officers, the payment of high salaries to officials, etc. Other determining factors are the opportunity or skill possessed in buying the raw materials used at an advantageous rate, the success with which the fluctuations in the prices of these materials are foreseen, and the wages paid to employees and their relative efficiency.

It is unnecessary to carry this discussion of the elements determining cost further. It only remains to mention that special care should be used in determining whether the articles compared are in reality identical. In many cases no amount of description will insure that the articles are alike in all particulars. The raw materials, though designated the same, may be of different qualities, the workmanship may vary, and, finally, there may be quite a difference as regards the item of finish, discoverable only after a personal examination by experts. The more complicated the article, the greater the opportunity for variation in these respects. It is for this reason that every effort was made to secure information for simple units.

As regards the important point of the proportion of the total cost ascribable to labor, it is also apparent that great possibilities for differences exist. Here the most important determining factors are not only the rates of wages paid and the efficiency of the employees, but the character of the equipment which has just been considered. The choice between the production of an article largely by manual labor, or by the use of machinery, the introduction of which requires the expenditure of a large sum of money, is often a difficult one. One manufacturer may decide upon the former method of production and another upon the latter, with the result that, though the total cost of production in the two may be nearly the same, the proportion of the cost going for labor will be widely different.

Chief interest in the present investigation attaches to the opportunity afforded of making comparisons between the conditions in this country and in Great Britain and Belgium as regards the total cost of production and the part for which the remuneration of labor is responsible. The problem of securing comparable units—that is, of finding establishments in the different countries making exactly the same articles—has been a difficult one, and complete success has not always been obtained. In practically all cases, however, information concerning substantially similar articles was secured, and an opportunity is therefore afforded of making a general comparison of the cost of production of the articles considered in the different countries. It is of course to be understood that, owing to the wide range of costs existing within each country as regards many articles, it is impossible, no matter how elaborate an investigation may be made, to give any one figure as representing the cost of production in a particular country. The information here given, therefore, must be considered only as showing the conditions obtaining in representative establishments. At the same time it is believed that the figures here given do represent in this general way the conditions as they exist in the countries considered as regards the total cost of production, and the proportion of this total going for labor.

With these explanations, a brief analysis of the data collected is now entered upon, in which the effort is made to indicate those units in the United States, Great Britain, and Belgium, which are the most similar, and for which a comparison can therefore be the more legitimately made.

Agricultural implements.—Taking up the various articles for which costs are given in the order of their presentation, it will be seen that quotations of costs obtained for planters' eye hoes in Great Britain, units Nos. 12 and 13, correspond almost exactly in description with units Nos. 4 and 5 for the United States. In the United States, the total cost of producing one dozen hoes of the character described was $1.91 and $1.96, of which the labor cost in transforming the materials was $0.61 and $0.63, respectively. Similar returns for the Great Britain units were: Total cost, $2.27 and $2.31; labor cost in transforming the materials, $0.89 and $0.91, respectively.

For spades, the second article under agricultural implements, information concerning products of practically identical descriptions in the United States, Belgium, and Great Britain was obtained in units Nos. 23, 24, 25, 27, and 28. The first three units are for the United States, and refer to the same spade, with the exception that different kinds of steel and qualities of handles were used in their manufacture. The total cost of producing one dozen of these spades was $5.50, $5.07, and $4.57, respectively. The labor cost in transforming the materials was in all three cases the same, $0.70, or 12.73, 13.81, and 15.32 per cent of the total cost. In Belgium, unit No. 27, the total cost was $4.35, of which the labor cost in transforming the materials was $1.27, or 29.20 per cent; and in Great Britain, unit No. 28, $4.50, of which the labor cost in transforming the materials was $1.70, or 37.78 per cent.

Boots and shoes.—In boots and shoes, the product is one giving room for great differences as regards workmanship and finish, and it was necessary, therefore, to secure information for a large number of units. The fact that American machinery is largely used in this industry in both Great Britain and Belgium insures that the process of manufacture can not be greatly different in the three countries, and thus presupposes a favorable basis for a comparison of conditions.

Selecting from among the numerous units those most nearly corresponding in description, the following quotations may be placed in comparison: Unit No. 69, Belgium, with units Nos. 56, 57, 58, and 59, representing the products of one establishment, and Nos. 63, 64, and 65, representing the products of a second establishment in the United States. The character of the unit here considered is that of cheap pegged workingmen's shoes. The total cost of producing one dozen pairs of shoes, as here reported, was $10.81 in Belgium, $11.58, $11.22, $10.50, and $10.20 in the first establishment in the United States, and $10.50, $9.90, and $9.18 in the second. The different returns for the same establishment represent different costs according as different qualities of materials were employed. The labor cost in transforming the materials in Belgium was $2.70, or 24.98 per cent of the total cost, a figure both absolutely and relatively higher than that for any of the United States units.

Other comparisons are those of the Great Britain unit No. 70 with units No. 43, 47, and 52 for the United States; Great Britian unit No. 71 with the United States units Nos. 29, 38, 39, 40, 45, and 54; and Great Britain unit No. 72 with United States units Nos. 30, 41, and 42. A considerable variation in the costs of production, which can be seen by reference to the detailed statements, is here seen. This is due to the fact that the information relates to shoes of a higher grade, and there is therefore greater opportunity for differences in the quality of the material and workmanship employed which can not be shown by a technical discription.

In the case of ladies' shoes, those units having the most similar descriptions are the Belgian unit No. 90, the Great Britain unit No. 93, and the United States units Nos. 83, 84, and 85; and the Great Britain units Nos. 91 and 92, and the United States units Nos. 73 and 82.

Brick.—The fact that the sizes of brick ordinarily used in the different countries vary makes any absolute comparisons of costs difficult. Considering those sizes which are the nearest alike, however, as units Nos. 99 and 100 for Belgium, and Nos. 95, 96, and 97 for the United States; and Nos. 101 and 102 for Great Britain and No. 98 for the United States, the figures would seem to indicate a considerably lower cost in Belgium than in the United States, or $1.35 and $1.40 per 1,000 brick against $4.95, $5.10, and $5; while the costs in Great Britain approximated those in the United States, or $3.77 and $4.87 per 1,000 brick against $4.35 in the United States.

A general examination of all of the units shows that the proportion of the total cost ascribable to labor for the most part varies between the limits of 40 and 60 per cent.

Men's clothing.—Data in regard to men's clothing were obtained with exceptional completeness. The great variation in the quality of the materials used in the manufacture of clothing and the character of the workmanship employed render it impossible to select particular units for comparison. The general range of costs and the proportion going for labor can be seen by examining the 75 units concerning which information was obtained.

Cotton goods.—In the industry of cotton goods, information was obtained concerning the costs of various kinds of standard cloths. Here, too, the nature of the units is such as to make it extremely difficult to secure comparable units. The instance in which success was more nearly secured is that of unit No. 194 for the United States and unit No. 198 for Great Britain. The cost of producing one yard of the cloth described, in the United States, was $0.0348, of which $0.0108 was for labor in transforming the materials, and in Great Britain $0.0397, of which $0.0119 was for labor in transforming the materials. The relative importance of the item of labor cost in the two countries was therefore nearly the same, being 31.03 per cent in the United States, and 29.97 per cent in Great Britain.

A fairly approximate similarity as regards description also exists in the case of the Great Britain unit No. 199 and the United States unit No. 180, the number of picks per inch being the same, 76x76, in both cases, and the number of yarn being 36 and 38 in the case of the Great Britain unit, and 28 and 40 in that of the United States. The total cost of producing one yard of this cloth in the United States was $0.0385, of which $0.0129 was for labor in transforming the materials, and in Great Britain $0.0308, of which $0.013 was for labor in transforming the materials. The greater cost in the United States is offset by the fact that the cloth in the case of the United States unit was 39 inches wide, while that for the Great Britain unit was but 36 inches.

Cutlery.—In the cutlery industry units were obtained for pocketknives, table knives, and table-knife blades. As there is greater opportunity in pocketknives for differences as regards workmanship and finish that can not be brought out by a verbal description, the best units for comparison are the simpler articles of table knives and table-knife blades. Units Nos. 242 to 249 represent data from four firms in the United States, and show the cost of manufacture of one dozen ivory-handled table knives of medium size to be $6.11, $5.55, and $4.96 in the first establishment; $6.04 in the second; $5.51, $4.73, and $2.94 in the third, and $8.12 in the fourth establishment. The different quotations of cost in the same establishment are due chiefly to the different grades of ivory used, as shown in the descriptions of the units. In contrast with these, units Nos. 269 and 270 show the cost of producing very similar articles in Great Britain to be $4.50 and $4.56, according to whether the blades were machine or hand made. Of this the labor cost in transforming the materials was $0.85 and $0.91, respectively. In the United States the labor cost in transforming the materials was $2.035, $1.30, $1.35, and $0.94 in the different establishments, respectively.

Probably the best basis for comparison, however, is to eliminate the item of the handle and consider the cost of making the blade alone. This is done in units Nos. 271 to 282 representing the United States; No. 283, Belgium, and Nos. 284 and 285, Great Britain. The last four units for the United States represent blades of the most ordinary quality intended for fitting into redwood handles, and therefore are not suitable for comparison with the Belgian and Great Britain products. The other units, however, represent blades closely approximating in character the Belgian and Great Britain units. The total cost of producing one dozen blades as described is shown by these units to be, in the United States, $0.875, $0.94, $1.28, $1.18, $1.06, $0.70, $0.84, and $0.80, respectively; in Belgium $0.4825, and in Great Britain $0.8516 and $0.9125 according to whether they were machine or hand made. The labor cost in transforming the materials was, in the United States. $0.70, $0.62, $1.02, $0.63, $0.55, $0.48, $0.60, and $0.57, respectively; in Belgium $0.386, and in Great Britain $0.4461 and $0.507.

Furniture.—In furniture units were secured for plain tables, dining tables, and bent-wood chairs. In regard to the first two articles a comparison of the Great Britain units, Nos. 290 and 294, with the units for the United States, Nos. 286 to 289 and 291 to 293, shows the cost of production to be materially less in the United States than in Great Britain. This smaller cost is found in both labor and other items. The cost of producing a plain oak table 42x42 inches in Great Britain was $3.67, as against $1.66 for a similar but somewhat smaller table, 24x42 inches in the United States, $1.72 for one 32x40 inches and $1.64 for a third 30x40 inches. The cost of the labor in transforming the materials was in the case of the Great Britain unit $1.14, and for the United States units $0.70, $0.63, and $0.49, respectively. In the case of dining tables the total cost was $6.67 in Great Britain, and for a similarly described table in the United States $3.99 in one case, $2.14 in a second, and $2.63 in a third.

As regards bent-wood chairs without arms, the cost of producing one dozen in Belgium was reported, unit No. 299, as $9.26, and in the United States, unit No. 296, as $8.54.

Glass.—In glass information concerning the cost of production of practically identical units in the United States and Great Britain was secured in the case of green glass pickle and green-glass spirit bottles. As regards the first article, unit No. 304 shows the cost of producing one gross of bottles in Great Britain to have been $2.49, of which $1.03 was for labor in transforming the materials. Returns from four firms in the United States for the same article, units Nos. 300 to 303, showed the total cost to have been $3.93, $2.97, $3.04, and $3.13, respectively, in which the cost of labor in transforming the materials figured for $1.63, $1.605, $1.60, and $1.88.

For green-glass spirit bottles the cost in Great Britain of one gross, unit No. 308, was $3.06, of which $1.15 was for labor in transforming the materials, while units Nos. 305, 306, and 307 give the total cost in the United States as $5.46, $4.13, and $3.75, of which $1.97, $1.88, and $2.26 was for labor in transforming the materials.

Men's hats.—Owing to the variety of styles and qualities of men's hats, a "medium" hat representative of each of the main classes of hats furnishes the best basis of comparison that can be obtained. This is due to the fact that the products of different establishments may describe the same and yet differ materially as regards the quality of material used or care with which they are finished.

For stiff, or derby, fur hats, units Nos. 317, 318, and 319, representing the cost of manufacture of cheap, medium, and fine grades of hats in Belgium, and units Nos. 320 and 321, representing the cost of medium and cheap grades of hats in Great Britain, may be placed in comparison with units Nos. 309 to 316 for the United States, care being taken to compare the same grades of hats in each case. The cost of the medium grade of hats in Belgium is given as $11.58 per dozen, of which $3.474 was for labor in transforming the materials; in Great Britain as from $8.52 to $9.73, of which from $2.92 to $3.24 was for labor in transforming the materials; and in the United States, in different establishments as $13.50, $14.75, and $11.22, of which $6.77, $8.25, and $6.63, respectively, was for labor in transforming the materials.

In like manner a somewhat similar comparison can be made as regards the cost of soft fur, soft wool, and flexible wool hats in the United States and in one or both of the foreign countries considered. It is, of course, understood that the average hat of one establishment may not be exactly the same as the average hat of another, and that the figures here given can only be considered as showing the general conditions as regards costs in the different establishments. It is believed, however, that the showing made is typical of conditions as they actually exist.

Iron and steel.—Information concerning the cost of representative products in the iron and steel industry was obtained for Great Britain and the United States only. The articles for which a comparison as regards their cost of production in the two countries can be made are cast-iron pipe, pig iron, and steel rails. Unit No. 347 shows the average cost of producing various sizes of cast-iron pipe in Great Britain to have been $21.29 per ton, of which $7.30 was for labor in transforming the materials. Units Nos. 344, 345, and 346 show the cost of producing an average size pipe. of 6, 4, and 3 inches in diameter, respectively, in the United States to have been $18.17, $19.17, and $20.17, respectively, of which $4.22, $5.22, and $6.22 was for labor in transforming the materials.

The cost of producing different kinds of pig iron in the United States is given, in units Nos. 348 to 356, as $9.60, $9.60, $10, $10.20, $9.21, $9.75, $8.87, $8.39, and $10.66, and in Great Britain, in units Nos. 357 and 358, as $9.73 and $12.04. In the United States the labor cost in transforming the materials was $0.60, $1.18, $0.80, $0.60, $0.73, $1, $0.60, $1.28, and $1.23, and in Great Britain $0.73 and $0.79.

As regards steel rails, the cost of producing 1 ton of this product was reported by two firms in Great Britain, units Nos. 361 and 362, to be $23.83 and $19.47, respectively, and by one firm in the United States, unit No. 359, as $18. It should be stated that the data for unit No. 361 represents an average for the five years 1890 to 1894, which probably accounts for its cost being shown as considerably greater than that given by the other Great Britain unit. In these two units the labor cost in transforming the materials is given as $3.67 and $1.95, and in the case of the United States unit as $2.70.

Leather.—The information for leather, particularly as regards those products other than sole leather, in Great Britain and Belgium was not obtained in a very satisfactory shape. The only comparison between conditions in the different countries that is feasible is, therefore, that of the tanning of sole leather from rawhide. Unit No. 364 gives the cost of tanning 1 hide, producing an average of 36 pounds of finished leather, in the United States as $10.14, of which $0.73 was for labor. Unit No. 368 gives the cost of tanning a hide, producing the same amount of finished sole leather, in Great Britain as $9.71, of which $1 was for labor. The Belgian unit No. 367, while not stating the amount of leather produced, gives the cost of tanning 1 hide at from $7.14 to $10.71, of which from $0.42 to $0.50 was for labor. Reference can be made to units Nos. 363, 365, and 366 as showing the cost of producing sole leather in other establishments in the United States.

Pottery products.—As representative products of the pottery industry information was obtained concerning the cost of producing ironstone china plates of different sizes and cups and saucers of the same material. As regards the figures of costs here given it should be stated that the manufacturers giving them said that, owing to the large variety of products manufactured at the same time, it was impossible to state accurately the cost of particular articles. The figures given, though based in each case upon a careful calculation, can not, therefore, be considered as other than estimates. The fact that there is shown a wide divergence between the estimates of two manufacturers in the United States doing business in the same city as regards the cost of substantially the same articles, would seem to indicate that a very close approximation to accuracy was not obtained. The two figures taken together, however, may represent the general range of costs. For the 8-inch plate, units Nos. 381 and 382, this cost for 1 dozen plates in the United States is given as $0.3801 and $0.4657, of which the labor cost in transforming the materials was $0.1233 and $0.2208. The returns for 1 dozen similar plates in Belgium and Great Britain, units Nos. 383 and 384, were, total cost, $0.6218 and $0.3649; labor cost in transforming the materials, $0.205 and $0.152. The extent to which these figures can be compared with those for the United States is subject to the limitations suggested by the observations given above.

Woolen goods.—There is probably no other important industry in which greater difficulties are experienced in the effort to secure information concerning the cost of producing particular articles, and especially of securing it in such a way that the products of different mills can be compared. The results of the present inquiry are given in units Nos. 390 to 446, inclusive, which show the cost of production of various kinds and grades of blankets, cloths, and yarns. As success in obtaining information for identical articles in the different countries was not attained, no effort is here made to place particular units in comparison. The general information concerning costs, however, is of value, but can best be obtained by consulting the detailed statements that follow. In interpreting this information as regards the United States, it is of great importance to take into consideration the element of time to which the figures of cost refer. The variations in the prices of raw wool and the scale of wages paid, due to tariff legislation and other causes, have necessarily affected materially the cost of production. Thus in the case of units Nos. 408, 409, and 421, representing the cost of producing the articles mentioned during the six months ending October 31, 1897, at one mill, it was reported by the official giving the information that subsequent to that period there had been an advance of 10 per cent in the cost of labor and 30 per cent in the cost of wool. In the same way for unit No. 414 the cost per yard is reported for November, 1897, as $0.1688 for labor in transforming the materials, $0.5812 for other items, and $0.75 as the total cost. The advance in the cost of labor and materials subsequent to November increased this cost on March 3, 1898, to the following figures: Labor in transforming the materials, $0.1857; other items, $0.7368; total cost, $0.9225, a very material increase. A similar increase was also reported in regard to unit No. 424, the total cost at the later date being stated as $0.193, as against but $0.14 in November, 1897.

While the other items in the detailed statement which follows can not be brought into very close comparison, they have an individual value in the study of the cost of production. They are, therefore, presented for what they are worth. The difficulty of securing exact descriptions of units, or so exact as to admit of comparison, has already been pointed out.

In submitting this report I take pleasure in acknowledging the valuable services, both in securing original data and in formulating comparisons, of Messrs. William F. Willoughby and Victor H. Olmsted, experts in the Department of Labor.

I am, very respectfully, your obedient servant,

CARROLL D. WRIGHT,
Commissioner.

Hon. GARRET A. HOBART,
Vice-President.

DETAILED STATEMENT OF THE LABOR COST IN TRANSFORMING MATERIALS AND TOTAL COST OF PRODUCTION OF CERTAIN ARTICLES IN THE UNITED STATES, GREAT BRITAIN, AND BELGIUM.

AGRICULTURAL IMPLEMENTS.

No. 1.—*Planters' eye hoes:* United States; 1897–98; unit, 1 dozen.
Size, No. 2, 7x8 inches; weight, 21¾ pounds per dozen; made in one solid piece of crucible hoe steel; polished halfway up the blade; eye and rib lacquered blue.

	Amount.	Per cent of total.
Cost of labor in transforming materials	$0.54	35.76
Cost of materials and all other items except labor	.97	64.24
Total cost	1.51	100.00

No. 2.—*Planters' eye hoes:* United States; 1897–98; unit, 1 dozen.
Size, No. 0, 6¼x7 inches; weight, 19 pounds per dozen; made of soft steel, faced with hardening steel halfway up front of blade; polished halfway up the blade; balance of hoe japanned black.

	Amount.	Per cent of total.
Cost of labor in transforming materials	$0.59	32.78
Cost of materials and all other items except labor	1.21	67.22
Total cost	1.80	100.00

No. 3.—*Planters' eye hoes:* United States; 1897–98; unit, 1 dozen.
Size, No. 1, 6½x7½ inches; weight, 22 pounds per dozen; of the same material and finish as product No. 2.

	Amount.	Per cent of total.
Cost of labor in transforming materials	$0.61	32.97
Cost of materials and all other items except labor	1.24	67.03
Total cost	1.85	100.00

No. 4.—*Planters' eye hoes:* United States; 1897–98; unit, 1 dozen.
Size, No. 2, 7x8 inches; weight, 25 pounds per dozen; of the same material and finish as product No. 2.

	Amount.	Per cent of total.
Cost of labor in transforming materials	$0.61	31.94
Cost of materials and all other items except labor	1.30	68.06
Total cost	1.91	100.00

No. 5.—*Planters' eye hoes:* United States; 1897-98; unit, 1 dozen.
Size, No. 3, 7¼x8¼ inches; weight, 28 pounds per dozen; of the same material and finish as product No. 2.

	Amount.	Per cent of total.
Cost of labor in transforming materials	$0.63	32.14
Cost of materials and all other items except labor	1.33	67.86
Total cost	1.96	100.00

No. 6.—*Planters' eye hoes:* United States; 1897-98; unit, 1 dozen.
Size, No. 4, 8x9 inches; weight, 31 pounds per dozen; of the same material and finish as product No. 2.

	Amount.	Per cent of total.
Cost of labor in transforming materials	$0.63	31.34
Cost of materials and all other items except labor	1.38	68.66
Total cost	2.01	100.00

No. 7.—*Planters' eye hoes:* United States; 1897-98; unit, 1 dozen.
Size, No. 0, 6¼x7 inches; weight, 18 pounds per dozen; made entirely of high-carbon steel, hardened and tempered; polished halfway up the blade; balance of hoe japanned black.

	Amount.	Per cent of total.
Cost of labor in transforming materials	$0.45	29.41
Cost of materials and all other items except labor	1.08	70.59
Total cost	1.53	100.00

No. 8.—*Planters' eye hoes:* United States; 1897-98; unit, 1 dozen.
Size, No. 1, 6½x7½ inches; weight, 20 pounds per dozen; of the same material and finish as product No. 7.

	Amount.	Per cent of total.
Cost of labor in transforming materials	$0.47	29.75
Cost of materials and all other items except labor	1.11	70.25
Total cost	1.58	100.00

No. 9.—*Planters' eye hoes:* United States; 1897-98; unit, 1 dozen.
Size, No. 2, 7x8 inches; weight, 21 pounds per dozen; of the same material and finish as product No. 7.

	Amount.	Per cent of total.
Cost of labor in transforming materials	$0.47	28.66
Cost of materials and all other items except labor	1.17	71.34
Total cost	1.64	100.00

No. 10.—*Planters' eye hoes:* United States; 1897–98; unit, 1 dozen.

Size, No. 3, 7½x8½ inches; weight, 21½ pounds per dozen; of the same material and finish as product No. 7.

	Amount.	Per cent of total.
Cost of labor in transforming materials	$0.50	29.76
Cost of materials and all other items except labor	1.18	70.24
Total cost	1.68	100.00

No. 11.—*Planters' eye hoes:* United States; 1897–98; unit, 1 dozen.

Size, No. 4, 8x9 inches; weight, 22½ pounds per dozen; of the same material and finish as product No. 7.

	Amount.	Per cent of total.
Cost of labor in transforming materials	$0.50	28.90
Cost of materials and all other items except labor	1.23	71.10
Total cost	1.73	100.00

No. 12.—*Planters' eye hoes:* Great Britain; 1897; unit, 1 dozen.

Size, No. 2, 7x8 inches; weight, 27 to 30 pounds per dozen; made of cheap basic steel, faced with hardening cast steel halfway up front of blade; entire blade polished; eye and rib japanned black.

	Amount.	Per cent of total.
Cost of labor in transforming materials	$0.89	39.21
Cost of materials and all other items except labor	1.38	60.79
Total cost	2.27	100.00

No. 13.—*Planters' eye hoes:* Great Britain; 1897; unit, 1 dozen.

Of the same size, weight, and finish as product No. 12, but made entirely of good Bessemer steel, hardened.

	Amount.	Per cent of total.
Cost of labor in transforming materials	$0.91	39.39
Cost of materials and all other items except labor	1.40	60.61
Total cost	2.31	100.00

No. 14.—*Spades:* United States; 1897; unit, 1 dozen.

Size of blade, 7¾x12¾ inches; weight 5¼ pounds; made of high-grade carbon steel, with double riveted D handles of best ash timber; blades treaded and polished on both sides.

	Amount.	Per cent of total.
Cost of labor in transforming materials	$1.85	39.36
Cost of materials and all other items except labor	2.85	60.64
Total cost	4.70	100.00

No. 15.—*Spades:* United States; 1897; unit, 1 dozen.

Of the same general description as product No. 14, but weighing 5 pounds, and made of lower grade of steel and poorer quality of timber.

	Amount.	Per cent of total.
Cost of labor in transforming materials	$1.85	42.53
Cost of materials and all other items except labor	2.50	57.47
Total cost	4.35	100.00

No. 16.—*Spades:* United States; 1897; unit, 1 dozen.

Size of blade, $7\frac{3}{16}$x12 inches; weight, $4\frac{3}{4}$ pounds; made of Bessemer steel, with double riveted D handles of cheap grade ash timber; blades treaded and polished on both sides.

	Amount.	Per cent of total.
Cost of labor in transforming materials	$1.50	42.86
Cost of materials and all other items except labor	2.00	57.14
Total cost	3.50	100.00

No. 17.—*Spades:* United States; 1897; unit, 1 dozen.

Size of blade, $7\frac{5}{8}$x12 inches; weight, 5 pounds; solid steel; smooth back pattern; made of high carbon Bessemer steel; tempered; with double riveted D handles of best ash timber; blades treaded or stepped, and full polished on both sides.

	Amount.	Per cent of total.
Cost of labor in transforming materials	$1.74	33.21
Cost of materials and all other items except labor	3.50	66.79
Total cost	5.24	100.00

No. 18.—*Spades:* United States; 1897; unit, 1 dozen.

Of same general description as product No. 17, but weighing $4\frac{1}{4}$ pounds; made of lower grade Bessemer steel, and with poorer quality of ash handles, and of less expensive finish.

	Amount.	Per cent of total.
Cost of labor in transforming materials	$1.68	38.53
Cost of materials and all other items except labor	2.68	61.47
Total cost	4.36	100.00

No. 19.—*Spades:* United States; 1897; unit, 1 dozen.

Size of blade, $7\frac{5}{8}$x12 inches; back strap spade having front and back strap riveted to the blade; made of low grade Bessemer steel, with double riveted D handles of low grade ash timber; black finish.

	Amount.	Per cent of total.
Cost of labor in transforming materials	$1.61	59.63
Cost of materials and all other items except labor	1.09	40.37
Total cost	2.70	100.00

No. 20.—*Spades:* United States: 1897; unit, 1 dozen.

Size of blade, 7¾x12 inches; hollow back or socket pattern spades, having the handle inserted into a socket formed from a portion of the blade and extending 9 inches above its top; made of low carbon Bessemer steel, with double riveted D handles of common ash timber; black finish.

	Amount.	Per cent of total.
Cost of labor in transforming materials	$0.78	32.50
Cost of materials and all other items except labor	1.62	67.50
Total cost	2.40	100.00

No. 21.—*Spades:* United States: 1897; unit, 1 dozen.

Of the same general description as product No. 20, but made of high carbon Bessemer steel, with good selected ash handles, and of better general finish.

	Amount.	Per cent of total.
Cost of labor in transforming materials	$0.78	21.02
Cost of materials and all other items except labor	2.93	78.98
Total cost	3.71	100.00

No. 22.—*Spades:* United States; 1897; unit, 1 dozen.

Of the same general description as product No. 20, but made of crucible cast steel, with handles of the best selected ash timber.

	Amount.	Per cent of total.
Cost of labor in transforming materials	$0.84	15.14
Cost of materials and all other items except labor	4.71	84.86
Total cost	5.55	100.00

No. 23.—*Spades:* United States; 1897–98; unit, 1 dozen.

Size of blade, edge, 7½ inches; shoulder, 7½ inches; length, 12 inches; weight, 5 pounds; "hollow back" or "open back" pattern, having the blade and socket for handle formed from one piece of steel, the handle being fitted into the socket thus formed; the top of the blade is bent back to form the tread; made of crucible steel, with double riveted D handles of ash timber.

	Amount.	Per cent of total.
Cost of labor in transforming materials	$0.70	12.73
Cost of materials and all other items except labor	4.80	87.27
Total cost	5.50	100.00

No. 24.—*Spades:* United States; 1897–98; unit, 1 dozen.

Of the same general description as product No. 23, but made of open-hearth steel.

	Amount.	Per cent of total.
Cost of labor in transforming materials	$0.70	13.81
Cost of materials and all other items except labor	4.37	86.19
Total cost	5.07	100.00

No. 25.—*Spades:* United States: 1897-98; unit, 1 dozen.
Of the same general description as product No. 23, but made of high-carbon Bessemer steel, and with a cheaper grade of ash handles.

	Amount.	Per cent of total.
Cost of labor in transforming materials	$0.70	15.32
Cost of materials and all other items except labor	3.87	84.68
Total cost	4.57	100.00

No. 26.—*Spades:* United States; 1897-98; unit, 1 dozen.
Of the same general description as product No. 23, but made of ordinary Bessemer steel, and with a cheaper grade of ash handles.

	Amount.	Per cent of total.
Cost of labor in transforming materials	$0.70	16.67
Cost of materials and all other items except labor	3.50	83.33
Total cost	4.20	100.00

No. 27.—*Spades:* Belgium; 1897; unit, 1 dozen.
Size of blade, 7¼x12 inches; "hollow-back" pattern, having blade and socket for handle formed from one piece of steel, handles being fitted into the socket thus formed; made of hard steel; handles of ash.

	Amount.	Per cent of total.
Cost of labor in transforming materials	$1.27	29.20
Cost of materials and all other items except labor	3.08	70.80
Total cost	4.35	100.00

No. 28.—*Spades:* Great Britain; 1897; unit, 1 dozen.
Size of blade No. 2, 7½x12 inches; weight, 5½ to 5¾ pounds; treaded; made of cheap basic steel, faced with hardened cast steel; polished from 3 to 4 inches up both sides; with double-riveted D handles of best ash timber.

	Amount.	Per cent of total.
Cost of labor in transforming materials	$1.70	37.78
Cost of materials and all other items except labor	2.80	62.22
Total cost	4.50	100.00

BOOTS AND SHOES.

No. 29.—*Men's shoes:* United States; 1897-98; unit, 1 dozen pairs.
Lace; all glazed, or vici, kid; leather lined; cap toe; Goodyear welt.

	Amount.	Per cent of total.
Cost of labor in transforming materials	$11.82	29.19
Cost of materials and all other items except labor	28.68	70.81
Total cost	40.50	100.00

No. 30.—*Men's shoes:* United States; 1897-98; unit, 1 dozen pairs.
Lace; French calf vamp; kid top; cap toe; Goodyear welt.

	Amount.	Per cent of total.
Cost of labor in transforming materials	$11.82	27.17
Cost of materials and all other items except labor	31.68	72.83
Total cost	43.50	100.00

No. 31.—*Men's shoes:* United States; 1897-98; unit, 1 dozen pairs.
Lace; wax calf vamp; kangaroo top; cloth lined; cap toe; Goodyear welt.

	Amount.	Per cent of total.
Cost of labor in transforming materials	$9.24	30.80
Cost of materials and all other items except labor	20.76	69.20
Total cost	30.00	100.00

No. 32.—*Men's shoes:* United States; 1897-98; unit, 1 dozen pairs.
Lace; wax calf vamp; kangaroo top; leather lined; cap toe; Goodyear welt.

	Amount.	Per cent of total.
Cost of labor in transforming materials	$9.24	29.24
Cost of materials and all other items except labor	22.36	70.76
Total cost	31.60	100.00

No. 33.—*Men's shoes:* United States; 1897-98; unit, 1 dozen pairs.
Lace; Russia calf top and vamp; leather lined; cap toe; Goodyear welt.

	Amount.	Per cent of total.
Cost of labor in transforming materials	$11.64	27.52
Cost of materials and all other items except labor	30.66	72.48
Total cost	42.30	100.00

No. 34.—*Men's shoes:* United States; 1897-98; unit, 1 dozen pairs.
Lace; Russia calf top and vamp; cloth lined; cap toe; Goodyear welt.

	Amount.	Per cent of total.
Cost of labor in transforming materials	$11.64	28.60
Cost of materials and all other items except labor	29.06	71.40
Total cost	40.70	100.00

No. 35.—*Men's shoes:* United States; 1897-98; unit, 1 dozen pairs.
Lace; willow calf vamp and top; leather lined; cap toe; Goodyear welt; very heavy double sole from heel to toe.

	Amount.	Per cent of total.
Cost of labor in transforming materials	$11.94	27.14
Cost of materials and all other items except labor	32.06	72.86
Total cost	44.00	100.00

No. 36.—*Men's shoes:* United States; 1897-98; unit, 1 dozen pairs.
Lace: patent calf vamp: kid top; cloth lined; cap toe; Goodyear welt.

	Amount.	Per cent of total.
Cost of labor in transforming materials	$12.72	30.37
Cost of materials and all other items except labor	29.16	69.63
Total cost	41.88	100.00

No. 37.—*Men's shoes:* United States; 1897-98; unit, 1 dozen pairs.
Lace; glazed or vici kid, top and vamp; straight cap; cloth lined; hand lasted; Goodyear welt.

	Amount.	Per cent of total.
Cost of labor in transforming materials	$10.04	32.68
Cost of materials and all other items except labor	20.68	67.32
Total cost	30.72	100.00

No. 38.—*Men's shoes:* United States; 1897-98; unit, 1 dozen pairs.
Lace; glazed or vici kid, top and vamp; straight cap; leather lined; hand lasted; Goodyear welt.

	Amount.	Per cent of total.
Cost of labor in transforming materials	$10.04	30.42
Cost of materials and all other items except labor	22.96	69.58
Total cost	33.00	100.00

No. 39.—*Men's shoes:* United States; 1897-98; unit, 1 dozen pairs.
Of the same general description as product No. 37; but made of cheaper material and machine lasted.

	Amount.	Per cent of total.
Cost of labor in transforming materials	$7.62	29.26
Cost of materials and all other items except labor	18.42	70.74
Total cost	26.04	100.00

No. 40.—*Men's shoes:* United States; 1897-98; unit, 1 dozen pairs.
Of the same general description as product No. 38; but made of cheaper material and machine lasted.

	Amount.	Per cent of total.
Cost of labor in transforming materials	$7.62	27.97
Cost of materials and all other items except labor	19.62	72.03
Total cost	27.24	100.00

No. 41.—*Men's shoes:* United States; 1897-98; unit, 1 dozen pairs.
Lace; kid top; calf vamp; straight cap; cloth lined; machine lasted; Goodyear welt.

	Amount.	Per cent of total.
Cost of labor in transforming materials	$9.08	30.39
Cost of materials and all other items except labor	20.80	69.61
Total cost	29.88	100.00

No. 42.—*Men's shoes:* United States; 1897–98; unit, 1 dozen pairs.
Of the same general description as product No. 41; but made of cheaper materials.

	Amount.	Per cent of total.
Cost of labor in transforming materials	$6.96	29.74
Cost of materials and all other items except labor	16.44	70.26
Total cost	23.40	100.00

No. 43.—*Men's shoes:* United States; 1897–98; unit, 1 dozen pairs.
Lace; dongola kid top; split vamp; leather lined; half double sole; McKay sewed.

	Amount.	Per cent of total.
Cost of labor in transforming materials	$6.30	33.33
Cost of materials and all other items except labor	12.60	66.67
Total cost	18.90	100.00

No. 44.—*Men's shoes:* United States; 1897–98; unit, 1 dozen pairs.
Lace; dongola kid top; calf vamp; canvas lined; half double sole; McKay sewed.

	Amount.	Per cent of total.
Cost of labor in transforming materials	$5.90	33.33
Cost of materials and all other items except labor	11.80	66.67
Total cost	17.70	100.00

No. 45.—*Men's shoes:* United States; 1897–98; unit, 1 dozen pairs.
Lace; glazed kid top and vamp; leather lined; Goodyear welt.

	Amount.	Per cent of total.
Cost of labor in transforming materials	$7.20	29.27
Cost of materials and all other items except labor	17.40	70.73
Total cost	24.60	100.00

No. 46.—*Men's shoes:* United States; 1897–98; unit, 1 dozen pairs.
Lace; kangaroo top; calf vamp; canvas lined; Goodyear welt.

	Amount.	Per cent of total.
Cost of labor in transforming materials	$7.20	32.88
Cost of materials and all other items except labor	14.70	67.12
Total cost	21.90	100.00

No. 47.—*Men's shoes:* United States; 1897–98; unit, 1 dozen pairs.
Lace; dongola kid top; split vamp; half double sole; McKay sewed.

	Amount.	Per cent of total.
Cost of labor in transforming materials	$4.44	37.00
Cost of materials and all other items except labor	7.56	63.00
Total cost	12.00	100.00

No. 48.—*Men's shoes:* United States; 1897-98; unit, 1 dozen pairs.
Lace; dongola kid top; calf vamp; canvas lined; half double sole; McKay sewed.

	Amount.	Per cent of total.
Cost of labor in transforming materials	$5.16	27.92
Cost of materials and all other items except labor	13.32	72.08
Total cost	18.48	100.00

No. 49.—*Men's shoes:* United States; 1897-98; unit, 1 dozen pairs.
Lace; dongola kid top; calf vamp; canvas lined; Goodyear welt.

	Amount.	Per cent of total.
Cost of labor in transforming materials	$7.20	34.09
Cost of materials and all other items except labor	13.92	65.91
Total cost	21.12	100.00

No. 50.—*Men's shoes:* United States; 1897-98; unit, 1 dozen pairs.
Lace; dongola kid top; satin (grain split) vamp; canvas lined; half double sole; McKay sewed.

	Amount.	Per cent of total.
Cost of labor in transforming materials	$4.44	31.90
Cost of materials and all other items except labor	9.48	68.10
Total cost	13.92	100.00

No. 51.—*Men's shoes:* United States; 1897-98; unit, 1 dozen pairs.
Lace; dongola kid top; satin (grain split) vamp; canvas lined; Goodyear welt.

	Amount.	Per cent of total.
Cost of labor in transforming materials	$6.48	39.13
Cost of materials and all other items except labor	10.08	60.87
Total cost	16.56	100.00

No. 52.—*Men's shoes:* United States; 1897-98; unit, 1 dozen pairs.
Lace; dongola kid top; split vamp; leather lined; half double sole; McKay sewed.

	Amount.	Per cent of total.
Cost of labor in transforming materials	$3.48	20.71
Cost of materials and all other items except labor	13.32	79.29
Total cost	16.80	100.00

No. 53.—*Men's shoes:* United States; 1897-98; unit, 1 dozen pairs.
Lace; dongola kid top; calf vamp; canvas lined; half double sole; McKay sewed.

	Amount.	Per cent of total.
Cost of labor in transforming materials	$4.56	24.20
Cost of materials and all other items except labor	14.28	75.80
Total cost	18.84	100.00

No. 54.—*Men's shoes:* United States; 1897-98; unit, 1 dozen pairs.
Lace; glazed kid top and vamp; straight cap; leather lined; Goodyear welt.

	Amount.	Per cent of total.
Cost of labor in transforming materials	$7.08	25.11
Cost of materials and all other items except labor	21.12	74.89
Total cost	28.20	100.00

No. 55.—*Men's shoes:* United States; 1897-98; unit, 1 dozen pairs.
Lace; dongola kid top; calf vamp; canvas lined; Goodyear welt.

	Amount.	Per cent of total.
Cost of labor in transforming materials	$6.60	29.89
Cost of materials and all other items except labor	15.48	70.11
Total cost	22.08	100.00

No. 56.—*Men's shoes:* United States; 1897-98; unit, 1 dozen pairs.
Lace; split upper; double sole; pegged; ordinary workingmen's shoes.

	Amount.	Per cent of total.
Cost of labor in transforming materials	$2.52	21.76
Cost of materials and all other items except labor	9.06	78.24
Total cost	11.58	100.00

No. 57.—*Men's shoes:* United States; 1897-98; unit, 1 dozen pairs.
Of the same general description and quality as product No. 56.

	Amount.	Per cent of total.
Cost of labor in transforming materials	$2.16	19.25
Cost of materials and all other items except labor	9.06	80.75
Total cost	11.22	100.00

No. 58.—*Men's shoes:* United States; 1897-98; unit, 1 dozen pairs.
Of the same general description as product No. 56, but made of cheaper materials.

	Amount.	Per cent of total.
Cost of labor in transforming materials	$2.16	20.57
Cost of materials and all other items except labor	8.34	79.43
Total cost	10.50	100.00

No. 59.—*Men's shoes:* United States; 1897-98; unit, 1 dozen pairs.
Of the same general description as product No. 56, but made of cheaper materials.

	Amount.	Per cent of total.
Cost of labor in transforming materials	$1.86	18.24
Cost of materials and all other items except labor	8.34	81.76
Total cost	10.20	100.00

No. 60.—*Men's shoes:* United States; 1897; unit, 1 dozen pairs.
Lace; heavy split first quality upper; half double sole; bellows tongue; pegged; workingmen's shoes known as "Western" tie.

	Amount.	Per cent of total.
Cost of labor in transforming materials	$2.37	21.47
Cost of materials and all other items except labor	8.67	78.53
Total cost	11.04	100.00

No. 61.—*Men's shoes:* United States; 1897; unit, 1 dozen pairs.
Of the same general description as product No. 60, but made of cheaper materials.

	Amount.	Per cent of total.
Cost of labor in transforming materials	$2.37	22.70
Cost of materials and all other items except labor	8.07	77.30
Total cost	10.44	100.00

No. 62.—*Men's shoes:* United States; 1897; unit, 1 dozen pairs.
Of the same general description as product No. 60, but made of cheaper materials.

	Amount.	Per cent of total.
Cost of labor in transforming materials	$2.37	24.09
Cost of materials and all other items except labor	7.47	75.91
Total cost	9.84	100.00

No. 63.—*Men's shoes:* United States; 1897–98; unit, 1 dozen pairs.
Lace; pegged; split upper; heavy workingmen's shoes.

	Amount.	Per cent of total.
Cost of labor in transforming materials	$2.28	21.71
Cost of materials and all other items except labor	8.22	78.29
Total cost	10.50	100.00

No. 64.—*Men's shoes:* United States; 1897–98; unit, 1 dozen pairs.
Of the same general description as product No. 63, but made of cheaper materials.

	Amount.	Per cent of total.
Cost of labor in transforming materials	$2.28	23.03
Cost of materials and all other items except labor	7.62	76.97
Total cost	9.90	100.00

No. 65.—*Men's shoes:* United States; 1897–98; unit, 1 dozen pairs.
Of the same general description as product No. 63, but made of cheaper materials.

	Amount.	Per cent of total.
Cost of labor in transforming materials	$2.28	24.84
Cost of materials and all other items except labor	6.90	75.16
Total cost	9.18	100.00

No. 66.—*Men's shoes:* United States; 1898; unit, 1 dozen pairs.
Lace; pegged; split upper; double sole; ordinary workingmen's shoes.

	Amount.	Per cent of total.
Cost of labor in transforming materials	$2.70	23.08
Cost of materials and all other items except labor	9.00	76.92
Total cost	11.70	100.00

No. 67.—*Men's shoes:* United States; 1898; unit, 1 dozen pairs.
Lace; pegged; kip upper; double sole; ordinary workingmen's shoes.

	Amount.	Per cent of total.
Cost of labor in transforming materials	$2.70	20.55
Cost of materials and all other items except labor	10.44	79.45
Total cost	13.14	100.00

No. 68.—*Men's shoes:* Belgium; 1897; unit, 1 dozen pairs.
Lace; dressed calf top; waxed calf vamp; sewed.

	Amount.	Per cent of total.
Cost of labor in transforming materials	$3.09	19.52
Cost of materials and all other items except labor	12.74	80.48
Total cost	15.83	100.00

No. 69.—*Men's shoes:* Belgium; 1897; unit, 1 dozen pairs.
Lace; waxed split calf upper; pegged; ordinary workingmen's shoes.

	Amount.	Per cent of total.
Cost of labor in transforming materials	$2.70	24.98
Cost of materials and all other items except labor	8.11	75.02
Total cost	10.81	100.00

No. 70.—*Men's shoes:* Great Britain; 1897; unit, 1 dozen pairs.
Lace; kid top; split vamp; leather lined; McKay sewed.

	Amount.	Per cent of total.
Cost of labor in transforming materials	$6.14	38.54
Cost of materials and all other items except labor	9.79	61.46
Total cost	15.93	100.00

No. 71.—*Men's shoes:* Great Britain; 1897; unit, 1 dozen pairs.
Lace; glazed kid top and vamp; straight cap; leather lined; Goodyear welt.

	Amount.	Per cent of total.
Cost of labor in transforming materials	$14.48	39.54
Cost of materials and all other items except labor	22.14	60.46
Total cost	36.62	100.00

No. 72.—*Men's shoes:* Great Britain; 1897; unit, 1 dozen pairs.
Lace; kid top; French calf vamp; cap; Goodyear welt.

	Amount.	Per cent of total.
Cost of labor in transforming materials	$13.18	39.13
Cost of materials and all other items except labor	20.50	60.87
Total cost	33.68	100.00

No. 73.—*Ladies' shoes:* United States; 1897-98; unit, 1 dozen pairs.
Lace; glacé kid; plain top and vamp; cloth and leather lined; Goodyear welt.

	Amount.	Per cent of total.
Cost of labor in transforming materials	$6.54	32.63
Cost of materials and all other items except labor	13.50	67.37
Total cost	20.04	100.00

No. 74.—*Ladies' shoes:* United States; 1897-98; unit, 1 dozen pairs.
Lace; glacé kid; plain top and vamp; cloth and leather lined; McKay sewed.

	Amount.	Per cent of total.
Cost of labor in transforming materials	$4.14	21.26
Cost of materials and all other items except labor	15.33	78.74
Total cost	19.47	100.00

No. 75.—*Ladies' shoes:* United States; 1897-98; unit, 1 dozen pairs.
Lace; glacé kid; cloth and leather lined; McKay sewed.

	Amount.	Per cent of total.
Cost of labor in transforming materials	$4.55	35.27
Cost of materials and all other items except labor	8.35	64.73
Total cost	12.90	100.00

No. 76.—*Ladies' shoes:* United States; 1897-98; unit, 1 dozen pairs.
Of the same general description as product No. 75, but made of better materials.

	Amount.	Per cent of total.
Cost of labor in transforming materials	$4.90	33.49
Cost of materials and all other items except labor	9.73	66.51
Total cost	14.63	100.00

No. 77.—*Ladies' shoes:* United States; 1897-98; unit, 1 dozen pairs.
Of the same general description as product No. 75, but made of better materials.

	Amount.	Per cent of total.
Cost of labor in transforming materials	$5.50	32.03
Cost of materials and all other items except labor	11.67	67.97
Total cost	17.17	100.00

No. 78.—*Ladies' shoes:* United States; 1897-98; unit, 1 dozen pairs.
Lace; glazed dongola (or glacé) kid; plain vamp and top; square kid tip; drill lined; leather top piece and insole; McKay sewed.

	Amount.	Per cent of total.
Cost of labor in transforming materials	$4.20	26.97
Cost of materials and all other items except labor	11.37	73.03
Total cost	15.57	100.00

No. 79.—*Ladies' shoes:* United States; 1897-98; unit, 1 dozen pairs.
Lace; glazed dongola (or glacé) kid; plain vamp and top; square kid tip; drill lined; leather top piece and insole; Goodyear welt.

	Amount.	Per cent of total.
Cost of labor in transforming materials	$5.49	29.09
Cost of materials and all other items except labor	13.38	70.91
Total cost	18.87	100.00

No. 80.—*Ladies' shoes:* United States; 1897; unit, 1 dozen pairs.
Lace; bright dongola (or glacé) kid; cloth and leather lined; patent-leather tip; McKay sewed.

	Amount.	Per cent of total.
Cost of labor in transforming materials	$4.08	21.16
Cost of materials and all other items except labor	15.20	78.84
Total cost	19.28	100.00

No. 81.—*Ladies' shoes:* United States; 1897; unit, 1 dozen pairs.
Of the same general description as product No. 80, but made of cheaper materials.

	Amount.	Per cent of total.
Cost of labor in transforming materials	$3.90	24.15
Cost of materials and all other items except labor	12.25	75.85
Total cost	16.15	100.00

No. 82.—*Ladies' shoes:* United States; 1897-98; unit, 1 dozen pairs.
Button; glacé kid; plain vamp and top; cloth and leather lined; Goodyear welt.

	Amount.	Per cent of total.
Cost of labor in transforming materials	$6.72	31.55
Cost of materials and all other items except labor	14.58	68.45
Total cost	21.30	100.00

No. 83.—*Ladies' shoes:* United States; 1897-98; unit, 1 dozen pairs.
Button; glacé kid; plain vamp and top; cloth and leather lined; McKay sewed.

	Amount.	Per cent of total.
Cost of labor in transforming materials	$4.32	20.84
Cost of materials and all other items except labor	16.41	79.16
Total cost	20.73	100.00

No. 84.—*Ladies' shoes:* United States; 1897–98; unit, 1 dozen pairs.
Button; glacé kid; cloth and leather lined; McKay sewed.

	Amount.	Per cent of total.
Cost of labor in transforming materials	$4.80	36.87
Cost of materials and all other items except labor	8.22	63.13
Total cost	13.02	100.00

No. 85.—*Ladies' shoes:* United States; 1897–98; unit, 1 dozen pairs.
Of the same general description as product No. 84, but made of better materials.

	Amount.	Per cent of total.
Cost of labor in transforming materials	$5.06	35.48
Cost of materials and all other items except labor	9.20	64.52
Total cost	14.26	100.00

No. 86.—*Ladies' shoes:* United States; 1897–98; unit, 1 dozen pairs.
Of the same general description as product No. 84, but made of better materials.

	Amount.	Per cent of total.
Cost of labor in transforming materials	$5.70	33.37
Cost of materials and all other items except labor	11.38	66.63
Total cost	17.08	100.00

No. 87.—*Ladies' shoes.*—United States; 1897–98; unit, 1 dozen pairs.
Button; glazed dongola (or glacé) kid; plain vamp and top; square kid tip; drill lined; leather top piece and insole; McKay sewed.

	Amount.	Per cent of total.
Cost of labor in transforming materials	$4.35	28.27
Cost of materials and all other items except labor	11.04	71.73
Total cost	15.39	100.00

No. 88.—*Ladies' shoes:* United States; 1897–98; unit, 1 dozen pairs.
Button; glazed dongola (or glacé) kid; plain vamp and top; square kid tip; drill lined; leather top piece and insole; Goodyear welt.

	Amount.	Per cent of total.
Cost of labor in transforming materials	$5.55	29.18
Cost of materials and all other items except labor	13.47	70.82
Total cost	19.02	100.00

No. 89.—*Ladies' shoes:* United States; 1897; unit, 1 dozen pairs.
Button; bright dongola (or glacé) kid; cloth and leather lined; patent-leather tip; McKay sewed.

	Amount.	Per cent of total.
Cost of labor in transforming materials	$4.32	26.47
Cost of materials and all other items except labor	12.00	73.53
Total cost	16.32	100.00

No. 90.—*Ladies' shoes:* Belgium; 1897; unit, 1 dozen pairs.
Button; dressed-calf top and vamp; sewed; an average quality of shoe.

	Amount.	Per cent of total.
Cost of labor in transforming materials	$3.47	26.05
Cost of materials and all other items except labor	9.85	73.95
Total cost	13.32	100.00

No. 91.—*Ladies' shoes:* Great Britain; 1897; unit, 1 dozen pairs.
Lace; glacé kid top and vamp; worked lace holes; Goodyear welt.

	Amount.	Per cent of total.
Cost of labor in transforming materials	$12.02	44.50
Cost of materials and all other items except labor	14.99	55.50
Total cost	27.01	100.00

No. 92.—*Ladies' shoes:* Great Britain; 1897; unit, 1 dozen pairs.
Button; glacé kid top and vamp; average quality of shoe.

	Amount.	Per cent of total.
Cost of labor in transforming materials	$8.76	33.33
Cost of materials and all other items except labor	17.52	66.67
Total cost	26.28	100.00

No. 93.—*Ladies' shoes:* Great Britain; 1897; unit, 1 dozen pairs.
Button; fancy vamp; poor quality kid; leather lined; McKay sewed.

	Amount.	Per cent of total.
Cost of labor in transforming materials	$5.43	38.27
Cost of materials and all other items except labor	8.76	61.73
Total cost	14.19	100.00

BRICK.

No. 94.—*Common red building brick:* United States; 1897; unit, 1,000.
Size, 8x4x2¼ inches.

	Amount.	Per cent of total.
Cost of labor in transforming materials	$2.33	54.95
Cost of materials and all other items except labor	1.91	45.05
Total cost	4.24	100.00

No. 95.—*Common red building brick:* United States; 1897–98; unit, 1,000.
Size, 7¾x3¾x2¼ inches.

	Amount.	Per cent of total.
Cost of labor in transforming materials	$1.93	38.99
Cost of materials and all other items except labor	3.02	61.01
Total cost	4.95	100.00

No. 96.—*Common red building brick:* United States; 1897; unit, 1,000. Size, 7¾x3⅝x2¼ inches.

	Amount.	Per cent of total.
Cost of labor in transforming materials	$1.98	38.82
Cost of materials and all other items except labor	3.12	61.18
Total cost	5.10	100.00

No. 97.—*Common red building brick:* United States; 1897; unit, 1,000. Size, 7¾x3⅝x2¼ inches.

	Amount.	Per cent of total.
Cost of labor in transforming materials	$2.00	40.00
Cost of materials and all other items except labor	3.00	60.00
Total cost	5.00	100.00

No. 98.—*Common red building brick:* United States; 1897; unit, 1,000. Size, 8¼x3¾x2⅝ inches.

	Amount.	Per cent of total.
Cost of labor in transforming materials	$2.35	54.02
Cost of materials and all other items except labor	2.00	45.98
Total cost	4.35	100.00

No. 99.—*Common red building brick:* Belgium; 1897; unit, 1,000. Size, 7.874x3.937x2.756 inches.

	Amount.	Per cent of total.
Cost of labor in transforming materials	$0.66	48.89
Cost of materials and all other items except labor	.69	51.11
Total cost	1.35	100.00

No. 100.—*Common red building brick:* Belgium; 1897; unit, 1,000. Size, 7.874x3.937x2.756 inches.

	Amount.	Per cent of total.
Cost of labor in transforming materials	$0.78	55.71
Cost of materials and all other items except labor	.62	44.29
Total cost	1.40	100.00

No. 101.—*Common red building brick:* Great Britain; 1897; unit, 1,000. Size, 9x4½x3 inches.

	Amount.	Per cent of total.
Cost of labor in transforming materials	$2.19	58.09
Cost of materials and all other items except labor	1.58	41.91
Total cost	3.77	100.00

No. 102.—*Common red building brick:* Great Britain; 1897; unit, 1,000. Size, 9x4½x3 inches.

	Amount.	Per cent of total.
Cost of labor in transforming materials	$2.03	41.68
Cost of materials and all other items except labor	2.84	58.32
Total cost	4.87	100.00

MEN'S CLOTHING.

No. 103.—*Men's sack suits:* United States; 1897; unit, 1 suit. Cheap quality cheviot.

	Amount.	Per cent of total.
Cost of labor in transforming materials	$0.92	24.47
Cost of materials and all other items except labor	2.84	75.53
Total cost	3.76	100.00

No. 104.—*Men's sack suits:* United States; 1897; unit, 1 suit. Cheviot.

	Amount.	Per cent of total.
Cost of labor in transforming materials	$1.17	24.63
Cost of materials and all other items except labor	3.58	75.37
Total cost	4.75	100.00

No. 105.—*Men's sack suits:* United States; 1897; unit, 1 suit. Black cheviot.

	Amount.	Per cent of total.
Cost of labor in transforming materials	$1.05	28.77
Cost of materials and all other items except labor	2.60	71.23
Total cost	3.65	100.00

No. 106.—*Men's sack suits:* United States; 1897; unit, 1 suit. Fancy all-wool cheviot.

	Amount.	Per cent of total.
Cost of labor in transforming materials	$1.25	26.48
Cost of materials and all other items except labor	3.47	73.52
Total cost	4.72	100.00

No. 107.—*Men's sack suits:* United States; 1897; unit, 1 suit. Fancy all wool cheviot.

	Amount.	Per cent of total.
Cost of labor in transforming materials	$1.30	23.77
Cost of materials and all other items except labor	4.17	76.23
Total cost	5.47	100.00

No. 108.—*Men's sack suits:* United States; 1897; unit, 1 suit.
Cheap worsted.

	Amount.	Per cent of total.
Cost of labor in transforming materials	$1.20	22.64
Cost of materials and all other items except labor	4.10	77.36
Total cost	5.30	100.00

No. 109.—*Men's sack suits:* United States; 1897; unit, 1 suit.
Medium-grade worsted.

	Amount.	Per cent of total.
Cost of labor in transforming materials	$1.90	27.38
Cost of materials and all other items except labor	5.04	72.62
Total cost	6.94	100.00

No. 110.—*Men's sack suits:* United States; 1897; unit, 1 suit.
Good worsted.

	Amount.	Per cent of total.
Cost of labor in transforming materials	$2.05	25.37
Cost of materials and all other items except labor	6.03	74.63
Total cost	8.08	100.00

No. 111.—*Men's sack suits:* United States; 1897; unit, 1 suit.
Cheap clay worsted.

	Amount.	Per cent of total.
Cost of labor in transforming materials	$1.28	25.45
Cost of materials and all other items except labor	3.75	74.55
Total cost	5.03	100.00

No. 112.—*Men's sack suits:* United States; 1897; unit, 1 suit.
Clay worsted.

	Amount.	Per cent of total.
Cost of labor in transforming materials	$1.93	24.25
Cost of materials and all other items except labor	6.03	75.75
Total cost	7.96	100.00

No. 113.—*Men's sack suits:* United States; 1897; unit, 1 suit.
Fine clay worsted.

	Amount.	Per cent of total.
Cost of labor in transforming materials	$2.36	21.18
Cost of materials and all other items except labor	8.78	78.82
Total cost	11.14	100.00

No. 114.—*Men's sack suits:* United States; 1897; unit, 1 suit. Fancy worsted.

	Amount.	Per cent of total.
Cost of labor in transforming materials	$1.54	21.78
Cost of materials and all other items except labor	5.53	78.22
Total cost	7.07	100.00

No. 115.—*Men's sack suits:* United States; 1897; unit, 1 suit. Fancy worsted.

	Amount.	Per cent of total.
Cost of labor in transforming materials	$1.83	23.64
Cost of materials and all other items except labor	5.91	76.36
Total cost	7.74	100.00

No. 116.—*Men's sack suits:* United States; 1897; unit, 1 suit. Fancy worsted.

	Amount.	Per cent of total.
Cost of labor in transforming materials	$1.95	21.43
Cost of materials and all other items except labor	7.15	78.57
Total cost	9.10	100.00

No. 117.—*Men's sack suits:* United States; 1897; unit, 1 suit. Fancy worsted.

	Amount.	Per cent of total.
Cost of labor in transforming materials	$2.14	22.11
Cost of materials and all other items except labor	7.54	77.89
Total cost	9.68	100.00

No. 118.—*Men's sack suits:* United States; 1897; unit, 1 suit. Fancy worsted.

	Amount.	Per cent of total.
Cost of labor in transforming materials	$1.73	25.78
Cost of materials and all other items except labor	4.98	74.22
Total cost	6.71	100.00

No. 119.—*Men's sack suits:* United States; 1897; unit, 1 suit. Fancy plaid worsted.

	Amount.	Per cent of total.
Cost of labor in transforming materials	$1.95	23.00
Cost of materials and all other items except labor	6.53	77.00
Total cost	8.48	100.00

No. 120.—*Men's sack suits:* United States; 1897; unit, 1 suit. Mixed cassimere.

	Amount.	Per cent of total.
Cost of labor in transforming materials	$0.82	32.93
Cost of materials and all other items except labor	1.67	67.07
Total cost	2.49	100.00

No. 121.—*Men's sack suits:* United States; 1897; unit, 1 suit. Mixed cassimere.

	Amount.	Per cent of total.
Cost of labor in transforming materials	$0.91	31.38
Cost of materials and all other items except labor	1.99	68.62
Total cost	2.90	100.00

No. 122.—*Men's sack suits:* United States; 1897; unit, 1 suit. Mixed cassimere.

	Amount.	Per cent of total.
Cost of labor in transforming materials	$0.96	29.54
Cost of materials and all other items except labor	2.29	70.46
Total cost	3.25	100.00

No. 123.—*Men's sack suits:* United States; 1897; unit, 1 suit. Fancy cassimere.

	Amount.	Per cent of total.
Cost of labor in transforming materials	$1.51	24.63
Cost of materials and all other items except labor	4.62	75.37
Total cost	6.13	100.00

No. 124.—*Men's sack suits:* United States; 1897; unit, 1 suit. Fancy all-wool cassimere.

	Amount.	Per cent of total.
Cost of labor in transforming materials	$1.48	25.83
Cost of materials and all other items except labor	4.25	74.17
Total cost	5.73	100.00

No. 125.—*Men's sack suits:* United States; 1897; unit, 1 suit. Low-grade tweed.

	Amount.	Per cent of total.
Cost of labor in transforming materials	$0.90	30.41
Cost of materials and all other items except labor	2.06	69.59
Total cost	2.96	100.00

No. 126.—*Men's sack suits:* United States; 1897; unit, 1 suit. Medium-grade tweed.

	Amount.	Per cent of total.
Cost of labor in transforming materials	$1.00	25.71
Cost of materials and all other items except labor	2.89	74.29
Total cost	3.89	100.00

No. 127.—*Men's sack suits:* United States; 1897; unit, 1 suit. Good-grade tweed.

	Amount.	Per cent of total.
Cost of labor in transforming materials	$1.45	27.67
Cost of materials and all other items except labor	3.79	72.33
Total cost	5.24	100.00

No. 128.—*Men's sack suits:* United States; 1897; unit, 1 suit. Cheap serge.

	Amount.	Per cent of total.
Cost of labor in transforming materials	$1.45	28.71
Cost of materials and all other items except labor	3.60	71.29
Total cost	5.05	100.00

No. 129.—*Men's sack suits:* United States; 1897; unit, 1 suit. Medium serge.

	Amount.	Per cent of total.
Cost of labor in transforming materials	$1.90	27.46
Cost of materials and all other items except labor	5.02	72.54
Total cost	6.92	100.00

No. 130.—*Men's sack suits:* United States; 1897; unit, 1 suit. Good serge.

	Amount.	Per cent of total.
Cost of labor in transforming materials	$2.00	24.60
Cost of materials and all other items except labor	6.13	75.40
Total cost	8.13	100.00

No. 131.—*Men's sack suits:* United States; 1897; unit, 1 suit. Blue flannel.

	Amount.	Per cent of total.
Cost of labor in transforming materials	$1.49	22.47
Cost of materials and all other items except labor	5.14	77.53
Total cost	6.63	100.00

No. 132.—*Men's sack suits:* United States; 1897; unit, 1 suit.
French diagonal.

	Amount.	Per cent of total.
Cost of labor in transforming materials	$2.20	22.49
Cost of materials and all other items except labor	7.58	77.51
Total cost	9.78	100.00

No. 133.—*Men's sack suits:* Belgium; 1897; unit, 1 suit.
Plain or fancy cheviot.

	Amount.	Per cent of total.
Cost of labor in transforming materials	$0.34	17.44
Cost of materials and all other items except labor	1.61	82.56
Total cost	1.95	100.00

No. 134.—*Men's sack suits:* Belgium; 1897; unit, 1 suit.
Cheviot.

	Amount.	Per cent of total.
Cost of labor in transforming materials	$0.40	16.95
Cost of materials and all other items except labor	1.96	83.05
Total cost	2.36	100.00

No. 135.—*Men's sack suits:* Belgium; 1897; unit, 1 suit.
Cheviot or worsted.

	Amount.	Per cent of total.
Cost of labor in transforming materials	$0.48	16.55
Cost of materials and all other items except labor	2.42	83.45
Total cost	2.90	100.00

No. 136.—*Men's sack suits:* Belgium; 1897; unit, 1 suit.
Cheviot or worsted.

	Amount.	Per cent of total.
Cost of labor in transforming materials	$0.51	15.04
Cost of materials and all other items except labor	2.88	84.96
Total cost	3.39	100.00

No. 137.—*Men's sack suits:* Belgium; 1897; unit, 1 suit.
Fancy cheviot or worsted.

	Amount.	Per cent of total.
Cost of labor in transforming materials	$0.58	15.14
Cost of materials and all other items except labor	3.25	84.86
Total cost	3.83	100.00

No. 138.—*Men's sack suits:* Belgium; 1897; unit, 1 suit.
Cheviot or worsted.

	Amount.	Per cent of total.
Cost of labor in transforming materials	$0.60	13.99
Cost of materials and all other items except labor	3.69	86.01
Total cost	4.29	100.00

No. 139.—*Men's sack suits:* Belgium; 1897; unit, 1 suit.
Cheviot or worsted.

	Amount.	Per cent of total.
Cost of labor in transforming materials	$0.65	13.71
Cost of materials and all other items except labor	4.09	86.29
Total cost	4.74	100.00

No. 140.—*Men's sack suits:* Belgium; 1897; unit, 1 suit.
Cheviot or worsted.

	Amount.	Per cent of total.
Cost of labor in transforming materials	$0.72	13.85
Cost of materials and all other items except labor	4.48	86.15
Total cost	5.20	100.00

No. 141.—*Men's sack suits:* Belgium; 1897; unit, 1 suit.
Cheviot or worsted.

	Amount.	Per cent of total.
Cost of labor in transforming materials	$0.82	14.46
Cost of materials and all other items except labor	4.85	85.54
Total cost	5.67	100.00

No. 142.—*Men's sack suits:* Belgium; 1897; unit, 1 suit.
Cheviot or worsted.

	Amount.	Per cent of total.
Cost of labor in transforming materials	$0.92	14.91
Cost of materials and all other items except labor	5.25	85.09
Total cost	6.17	100.00

No. 143.—*Men's sack suits:* Belgium; 1897; unit, 1 suit.
Cheviot or worsted.

	Amount.	Per cent of total.
Cost of labor in transforming materials	$1.00	14.64
Cost of materials and all other items except labor	5.83	85.36
Total cost	6.83	100.00

No. 144.—*Men's sack suits:* Great Britain; 1897; unit, 1 suit.
Worsted; poor quality of trimmings and low-grade labor.

	Amount.	Per cent of total.
Cost of labor in transforming materials	$1.56	32.91
Cost of materials and all other items except labor	3.18	67.09
Total cost	4.74	100.00

No. 145.—*Men's sack suits:* Great Britain; 1897; unit, 1 suit.
Worsted; medium quality of trimmings and medium-grade labor.

	Amount.	Per cent of total.
Cost of labor in transforming materials	$2.05	29.58
Cost of materials and all other items except labor	4.88	70.42
Total cost	6.93	100.00

No. 146.—*Men's sack suits:* Great Britain; 1897; unit, 1 suit.
Worsted; good quality of trimmings and high-grade labor.

	Amount.	Per cent of total.
Cost of labor in transforming materials	$2.82	29.72
Cost of materials and all other items except labor	6.67	70.28
Total cost	9.49	100.00

No. 147.—*Men's sack suits:* Great Britain; 1897; unit, 1 suit.
Serge; poor quality of trimmings and low-grade labor.

	Amount.	Per cent of total.
Cost of labor in transforming materials	$1.56	32.91
Cost of materials and all other items except labor	3.18	67.09
Total cost	4.74	100.00

No. 148.—*Men's sack suits:* Great Britain; 1897; unit, 1 suit.
Serge; medium quality of trimmings and medium-grade labor.

	Amount.	Per cent of total.
Cost of labor in transforming materials	$2.05	29.58
Cost of materials and all other items except labor	4.88	70.42
Total cost	6.93	100.00

No. 149.—*Men's sack suits:* Great Britain; 1897; unit, 1 suit.
Serge; good quality of trimmings and high-grade labor.

	Amount.	Per cent of total.
Cost of labor in transforming materials	$2.82	29.72
Cost of materials and all other items except labor	6.67	70.28
Total cost	9.49	100.00

No. 150.—*Men's sack suits:* Great Britain; 1897; unit, 1 suit.
Tweed; poor quality of trimmings and low-grade labor.

	Amount.	Per cent of total.
Cost of labor in transforming materials	$1.56	32.91
Cost of materials and all other items except labor	3.18	67.09
Total cost	4.74	100.00

No. 151.—*Men's sack suits:* Great Britain; 1897; unit, 1 suit.
Tweed; medium quality of trimmings and medium-grade labor.

	Amount.	Per cent of total.
Cost of labor in transforming materials	$2.05	29.58
Cost of materials and all other items except labor	4.88	70.42
Total cost	6.93	100.00

No. 152.—*Men's sack suits:* Great Britain; 1897; unit, 1 suit.
Tweed; good quality of trimmings and high-grade labor.

	Amount.	Per cent of total.
Cost of labor in transforming materials	$2.82	29.72
Cost of materials and all other items except labor	6.67	70.28
Total cost	9.49	100.00

No. 153.—*Men's overcoats:* United States; 1897; unit, 1 coat.
Blue kersey.

	Amount.	Per cent of total.
Cost of labor in transforming materials	$0.90	25.64
Cost of materials and all other items except labor	2.61	74.36
Total cost	3.51	100.00

No. 154.—*Men's overcoats:* United States; 1897; unit, 1 coat.
Good quality kersey.

	Amount.	Per cent of total.
Cost of labor in transforming materials	$2.40	25.16
Cost of materials and all other items except labor	7.14	74.84
Total cost	9.54	100.00

No. 155.—*Men's overcoats:* United States; 1897; unit, 1 coat.
All-wool blue kersey.

	Amount.	Per cent of total.
Cost of labor in transforming materials	$1.50	28.68
Cost of materials and all other items except labor	3.73	71.32
Total cost	5.23	100.00

No. 156.—*Men's overcoats:* United States; 1897; unit, 1 coat.
Fine brown kersey.

	Amount.	Per cent of total.
Cost of labor in transforming materials	$1.85	22.48
Cost of materials and all other items except labor	6.38	77.52
Total cost	8.23	100.00

No. 157.—*Men's overcoats:* United States; 1897; unit, 1 coat.
Cheap black beaver.

	Amount.	Per cent of total.
Cost of labor in transforming materials	$1.10	31.34
Cost of materials and all other items except labor	2.41	68.66
Total cost	3.51	100.00

No. 158.—*Men's overcoats:* United States; 1897; unit, 1 coat.
Blue beaver.

	Amount.	Per cent of total.
Cost of labor in transforming materials	$1.00	21.05
Cost of materials and all other items except labor	3.75	78.95
Total cost	4.75	100.00

No. 159.—*Men's overcoats:* United States; 1897; unit, 1 coat.
Union beaver.

	Amount.	Per cent of total.
Cost of labor in transforming materials	$0.82	20.05
Cost of materials and all other items except labor	3.27	79.95
Total cost	4.09	100.00

No. 160.—*Men's overcoats:* United States; 1897; unit, 1 coat.
Patent beaver.

	Amount.	Per cent of total.
Cost of labor in transforming materials	$2.10	20.71
Cost of materials and all other items except labor	8.04	79.29
Total cost	10.14	100.00

No. 161.—*Men's overcoats:* United States; 1897; unit, 1 coat.
Patent beaver.

	Amount.	Per cent of total.
Cost of labor in transforming materials	$2.40	17.47
Cost of materials and all other items except labor	11.34	82.53
Total cost	13.74	100.00

No. 162.—*Men's overcoats:* United States; 1897; unit, 1 coat. Chinchilla.

	Amount.	Per cent of total.
Cost of labor in transforming materials	$1.15	22.64
Cost of materials and all other items except labor	3.93	77.36
Total cost	5.08	100.00

No. 163.—*Men's overcoats:* United States; 1897; unit, 1 coat. Blue chinchilla.

	Amount.	Per cent of total.
Cost of labor in transforming materials	$1.90	21.71
Cost of materials and all other items except labor	6.85	78.29
Total cost	8.75	100.00

No. 164.—*Men's overcoats:* United States; 1897; unit, 1 coat. Cheap chinchilla.

	Amount.	Per cent of total.
Cost of labor in transforming materials	$0.62	24.31
Cost of materials and all other items except labor	1.93	75.69
Total cost	2.55	100.00

No. 165.—*Men's overcoats:* United States; 1897; unit, 1 coat. Fine chinchilla.

	Amount.	Per cent of total.
Cost of labor in transforming materials	$2.70	23.16
Cost of materials and all other items except labor	8.96	76.84
Total cost	11.66	100.00

No. 166.—*Men's overcoats:* United States; 1897; unit, 1 coat. Blue melton.

	Amount.	Per cent of total.
Cost of labor in transforming materials	$1.40	22.26
Cost of materials and all other items except labor	4.89	77.74
Total cost	6.29	100.00

No. 167.—*Men's overcoats:* United States; 1897; unit, 1 coat. Blue melton.

	Amount.	Per cent of total.
Cost of labor in transforming materials	$1.50	21.07
Cost of materials and all other items except labor	5.62	78.93
Total cost	7.12	100.00

No. 168.—*Men's overcoats:* United States; 1897; unit, 1 coat.
Shoddy satinet.

	Amount.	Per cent of total.
Cost of labor in transforming materials	$0.55	27.09
Cost of materials and all other items except labor	1.48	72.91
Total cost	2.03	100.00

No. 169.—*Men's overcoats:* United States; 1897; unit, 1 coat.
Fine montagnac.

	Amount.	Per cent of total.
Cost of labor in transforming materials	$2.40	20.91
Cost of materials and all other items except labor	9.08	79.09
Total cost	11.48	100.00

No. 170.—*Men's overcoats:* Belgium; 1897; unit, 1 coat.
Beaver or cheviot.

	Amount.	Per cent of total.
Cost of labor in transforming materials	$0.39	21.08
Cost of materials and all other items except labor	1.46	78.92
Total cost	1.85	100.00

No. 171.—*Men's overcoats:* Belgium; 1897; unit, 1 coat.
Beaver.

	Amount.	Per cent of total.
Cost of labor in transforming materials	$0.53	23.25
Cost of materials and all other items except labor	1.75	76.75
Total cost	2.28	100.00

No. 172.—*Men's overcoats:* Belgium; 1897; unit, 1 coat.
Worsted.

	Amount.	Per cent of total.
Cost of labor in transforming materials	$0.63	23.51
Cost of materials and all other items except labor	2.05	76.49
Total cost	2.68	100.00

No. 173.—*Men's overcoats:* Belgium; 1897; unit, 1 coat.
Beaver or worsted.

	Amount.	Per cent of total.
Cost of labor in transforming materials	$0.63	19.69
Cost of materials and all other items except labor	2.57	80.31
Total cost	3.20	100.00

No. 174.—*Men's overcoats:* Belgium; 1897; unit, 1 coat.
Beaver, cheviot, or worsted.

	Amount.	Per cent of total.
Cost of labor in transforming materials	$0.72	19.89
Cost of materials and all other items except labor	2.90	80.11
Total cost	3.62	100.00

No. 175.—*Men's overcoats:* Belgium; 1897; unit, 1 coat.
Beaver, worsted, or covert cloth.

	Amount.	Per cent of total.
Cost of labor in transforming materials	$0.82	20.76
Cost of materials and all other items except labor	3.13	79.24
Total cost	3.95	100.00

No. 176.—*Men's overcoats:* Belgium; 1897; unit, 1 coat.
Beaver or worsted.

	Amount.	Per cent of total.
Cost of labor in transforming materials	$0.82	19.62
Cost of materials and all other items except labor	3.36	80.38
Total cost	4.18	100.00

No. 177.—*Men's overcoats:* Belgium; 1897; unit, 1 coat.
Beaver or fancy worsted.

	Amount.	Per cent of total.
Cost of labor in transforming materials	$1.01	20.08
Cost of materials and all other items except labor	4.02	79.92
Total cost	5.03	100.00

COTTON GOODS.

No. 178.—*Cloth:* United States; 1897; unit, 1 yard.
Twills; 37 inches wide; picks per inch, 80x60; warp yarn, No. 12; weft yarn, No. 13; 1.73 yards per pound.

	Amount.	Per cent of total.
Cost of labor in transforming materials	$0.0162	23.75
Cost of materials and all other items except labor	.0520	76.25
Total cost	.0682	100.00

No. 179.—*Cloth:* United States; 1897; unit, 1 yard.
Twills; 39 inches wide; picks per inch, 96x104; warp yarn, No. 34; weft yarn, No. 45; 3.80 yards per pound.

	Amount.	Per cent of total.
Cost of labor in transforming materials	$0.0257	39.06
Cost of materials and all other items except labor	.0401	60.94
Total cost	.0658	100.00

No. 180.—*Cloth:* United States; 1897-98; unit, 1 yard.

Four-leaf twills; 39 inches wide; picks per inch, 76x76; warp yarn, No. 28; weft yarn, No. 40; 4.25 yards per pound.

	Amount.	Per cent of total.
Cost of labor in transforming materials	$0.0129	33.51
Cost of materials and all other items except labor	.0256	66.49
Total cost	.0385	100.00

No. 181.—*Cloth:* United States; 1898; unit, 1 yard.

Four-leaf twills; 43 inches wide; picks per inch, 68x68; warp yarn, average number, 28.05; weft yarn, average number, 37.78; 4.30 yards per pound.

	Amount.	Per cent of total.
Cost of labor in transforming materials	$0.0134	35.64
Cost of materials and all other items except labor	.0242	64.36
Total cost	.0376	100.00

No. 182.—*Cloth:* United States; 1897-98; unit, 1 yard.

Five harvers Albert twills; 36 inches wide; picks per inch, 76x68; warp yarn, No. 30; weft yarn, No. 40; 5 yards per pound.

	Amount.	Per cent of total.
Cost of labor in transforming materials	$0.0115	37.10
Cost of materials and all other items except labor	.0195	62.90
Total cost	.0310	100.00

No. 183.—*Cloth:* United States; 1897; unit, 1 yard.

Twills or drills; 29 inches wide; picks per inch, 72x48; warp yarn, No. 12; weft yarn, No. 18; 2.85 yards per pound.

	Amount.	Per cent of total.
Cost of labor in transforming materials	$0.0114	25.50
Cost of materials and all other items except labor	.0333	74.50
Total cost	.0447	100.00

No. 184.—*Cloth:* United States; 1897-98; unit, 1 yard.

Twills or drills; 30 inches wide; picks per inch, 68x48; warp yarn, No. 14; weft yarn, No. 14; 2.85 yards per pound.

	Amount.	Per cent of total.
Cost of labor in transforming materials	$0.0113	28.25
Cost of materials and all other items except labor	.0287	71.75
Total cost	.0400	100.00

No. 185.—*Cloth:* United States; 1897-98; unit, 1 yard.

Percale; 39 inches wide; picks per inch, 72x62; warp yarn, No. 28; weft yarn, No. 46; 4.75 yards per pound.

	Amount.	Per cent of total.
Cost of labor in transforming materials	$0.0158	42.93
Cost of materials and all other items except labor	.0210	57.07
Total cost	.0368	100.00

No. 186.—*Cloth:* United States; 1897-98; unit, 1 yard.
Percale; 39 inches wide; picks per inch, 80x88; warp yarn, No. 40; weft yarn, No. 50; 4.75 yards per pound.

	Amount.	Per cent of total.
Cost of labor in transforming materials	$0.0180	43.37
Cost of materials and all other items except labor	.0235	56.63
Total cost	.0415	100.00

No. 187.—*Cloth:* United States; 1897-98; unit, 1 yard.
Percale; 39 inches wide; picks per inch, 88x92; warp yarn, No. 40; weft yarn, No. 64; 5 yards per pound.

	Amount.	Per cent of total.
Cost of labor in transforming materials	$0.0199	45.75
Cost of materials and all other items except labor	.0236	54.25
Total cost	.0435	100.00

No. 188.—*Cloth:* United States; 1897; unit, 1 yard.
Plain; 40 inches wide; picks per inch, 80x80; warp yarn, No. 60; weft yarn, No. 85; 8 yards per pound.

	Amount.	Per cent of total.
Cost of labor in transforming materials	$0.0275	45.16
Cost of materials and all other items except labor	.0334	54.84
Total cost	.0609	100.00

No. 189.—*Cloth:* United States; 1898; unit, 1 yard.
Plain; 35 inches wide; picks per inch, 68x72; warp yarn, No. 27½; weft yarn, No. 37¾; 5 yards per pound.

	Amount.	Per cent of total.
Cost of labor in transforming materials	$0.0116	35.69
Cost of materials and all other items except labor	.0209	64.31
Total cost	.0325	100.00

No. 190.—*Cloth:* United States; 1897-98; unit, 1 yard.
38½ inches wide; picks per inch, 64x64; warp yarn, No. 30; weft yarn, No. 36; 5.15 yards per pound.

	Amount.	Per cent of total.
Cost of labor in transforming materials	$0.0093	33.45
Cost of materials and all other items except labor	.0185	66.55
Total cost	.0278	100.00

No. 191.—*Cloth:* United States; 1897; unit, 1 yard.
39 inches wide; picks per inch, 68x72; warp yarn, No. 28; weft yarn, No. 40; 4.75 yards per pound.

	Amount.	Per cent of total.
Cost of labor in transforming materials	$0.0137	38.81
Cost of materials and all other items except labor	.0216	61.19
Total cost	.0353	100.00

No. 192.—*Cloth:* United States; 1897; unit, 1 yard.
28 inches wide; picks per inch, 64x64; warp yarn, No. 28; weft yarn, No. 36; 7 yards per pound.

	Amount.	Per cent of total.
Cost of labor in transforming materials	$0.0089	38.20
Cost of materials and all other items except labor	.0144	61.80
Total cost	.0233	100.00

No. 193.—*Cloth:* United States; 1898; unit, 1 yard.
28 inches wide; picks per inch, 64x64; warp yarn, No. 28; weft yarn, No. 38; 7 yards per pound.

	Amount.	Per cent of total.
Cost of labor in transforming materials	$0.0079	32.51
Cost of materials and all other items except labor	.0164	67.49
Total cost	.0243	100.00

No. 194.—*Cloth:* United States; 1898; unit, 1 yard.
35 inches wide; picks per inch, 76x72; average number of yarn used in warp and weft, 30; 4.42 yards per pound.

	Amount.	Per cent of total.
Cost of labor in transforming materials	$0.0108	31.03
Cost of materials and all other items except labor	.0240	68.97
Total cost	.0348	100.00

No. 195.—*Cloth:* United States; 1897; unit, 1 yard.
40 inches wide; picks per inch, 80x84; warp yarn, No. 28; weft yarn, No. 43; 3.90 yards per pound.

	Amount.	Per cent of total.
Cost of labor in transforming materials	$0.0182	35.48
Cost of materials and all other items except labor	.0331	64.52
Total cost	.0513	100.00

No. 196.—*Cloth:* United States; 1897; unit, 1 yard.
40 inches wide; picks per inch, 64x68; warp yarn, No. 19½; weft yarn, No. 24½; 3.50 yards per pound.

	Amount.	Per cent of total.
Cost of labor in transforming materials	$0.0136	28.10
Cost of materials and all other items except labor	.0348	71.90
Total cost	.0484	100.00

No. 197.—*Cloth:* United States; 1897-98; unit, 1 yard.
Sheeting; 36 inches wide; picks per inch, 62x62; warp yarn, No. 20; weft yarn, No. 22; 3.50 yards per pound.

	Amount.	Per cent of total.
Cost of labor in transforming materials	$0.0130	34.85
Cost of materials and all other items except labor	.0243	65.15
Total cost	.0373	100.00

No. 198.—*Cloth:* Great Britain; 1897; unit, 1 yard.
35 inches wide; picks per inch, 76x72; warp yarn, No. 30; weft yarn. No. 30.

	Amount.	Per cent of total.
Cost of labor in transforming materials	$0.0119	29.97
Cost of materials and all other items except labor	.0278	70.03
Total cost	.0397	100.00

No. 199.—*Cloth:* Great Britain; 1897; unit, 1 yard.
36 inches wide; picks per inch, 76x76; warp yarn, No. 36; weft yarn, No. 38.

	Amount.	Per cent of total.
Cost of labor in transforming materials	$0.0130	42.21
Cost of materials and all other items except labor	.0178	57.79
Total cost	.0308	100.00

CUTLERY.

No. 200.—*Pocketknives:* United States; 1897; unit, 1 dozen.
Pearl handle; Congress pattern; 3¼ inches long; medium German-silver bolsters; brass lined; 2 blades of English Wardlow steel.

	Amount.	Per cent of total.
Cost of labor in transforming materials	$3.41	53.20
Cost of materials and all other items except labor	3.00	46.80
Total cost	6.41	100.00

No. 201.—*Pocketknives:* United States; 1897; unit, 1 dozen.
Of the same general description as product No. 200, but having 4 blades.

	Amount.	Per cent of total.
Cost of labor in transforming materials	$4.95	61.04
Cost of materials and all other items except labor	3.16	38.96
Total cost	8.11	100.00

No. 202.—*Pocketknives:* United States; 1897; unit, 1 dozen.
Pearl handle; Senator pattern; 3¼ inches long; ¼-inch German-silver bolsters; German-silver lined; 4 blades of Thos. Firths & Sons English blade steel.

	Amount.	Per cent of total.
Cost of labor in transforming materials	$5.36	51.84
Cost of materials and all other items except labor	4.98	48.16
Total cost	10.34	100.00

No. 203.—*Pocketknives:* United States; 1897; unit, 1 dozen.
Pearl handle; Senator pattern; 3¼ inches long; ⅛-inch German-silver bolsters; brass lined; 2 blades of Thos. Firths & Sons English blade steel.

	Amount.	Per cent of total.
Cost of labor in transforming materials	$2.42	48.50
Cost of materials and all other items except labor	2.57	51.50
Total cost	4.99	100.00

No. 204.—*Pocketknives:* United States; 1897; unit, 1 dozen.
Of the same general description as product No. 203, but having 4 blades.

	Amount.	Per cent of total.
Cost of labor in transforming materials	$3.98	55.20
Cost of materials and all other items except labor	3.23	44.80
Total cost	7.21	100.00

No. 205.—*Pocketknives:* United States; 1897-98; unit, 1 dozen.
Pearl handle; Senator pattern; 3¼ inches long; ½-inch German-silver bolsters; brass lined; 2 blades of forged English Wardlow steel.

	Amount.	Per cent of total.
Cost of labor in transforming materials	$3.98	60.03
Cost of materials and all other items except labor	2.65	39.97
Total cost	6.63	100.00

No. 206.—*Pocketknives:* United States; 1897-98; unit, 1 dozen.
Of the same general description as product No. 205, but having 4 blades.

	Amount.	Per cent of total.
Cost of labor in transforming materials	$4.63	56.05
Cost of materials and all other items except labor	3.63	43.95
Total cost	8.26	100.00

No. 207.—*Pocketknives:* United States; 1897; unit, 1 dozen.
Ivory handle; Senator pattern; 3 inches long; medium German-silver bolsters; brass lined; 2 blades of English Wardlow steel.

	Amount.	Per cent of total.
Cost of labor in transforming materials	$2.36	76.87
Cost of materials and all other items except labor	.71	23.13
Total cost	3.07	100.00

No. 208.—*Pocketknives:* United States; 1897; unit, 1 dozen.
Of the same general description as product No. 207, but having 4 blades.

	Amount.	Per cent of total.
Cost of labor in transforming materials	$4.18	82.45
Cost of materials and all other items except labor	.89	17.55
Total cost	5.07	100.00

No. 209.—*Pocketknives:* United States; 1897; unit, 1 dozen.
Ivory handle; Senator pattern; 3 inches long; ⅜-inch German-silver bolsters; brass lined; 2 blades of Thos. Firths & Sons' English blade steel.

	Amount.	Per cent of total.
Cost of labor in transforming materials	$2.21	61.90
Cost of materials and all other items except labor	1.36	38.10
Total cost	3.57	100.00

No. 210.—*Pocketknives:* United States; 1897; unit, 1 dozen.
Of the same general description as product No. 209, but having 4 blades.

	Amount.	Per cent of total.
Cost of labor in transforming materials	$3.60	67.54
Cost of materials and all other items except labor	1.73	32.46
Total cost	5.33	100.00

No. 211.—*Pocketknives:* United States; 1897-98; unit, 1 dozen.
Ivory handle; Senator pattern; 3 inches long; ¼-inch German-silver bolsters; brass lined; 2 blades of forged English Wardlow steel.

	Amount.	Per cent of total.
Cost of labor in transforming materials	$2.89	72.43
Cost of materials and all other items except labor	1.10	27.57
Total cost	3.99	100.00

No. 212.—*Pocketknives:* United States; 1897-98; unit, 1 dozen.
Of the same general description as product No. 211, but having 4 blades.

	Amount.	Per cent of total.
Cost of labor in transforming materials	$3.49	66.73
Cost of materials and all other items except labor	1.74	33.27
Total cost	5.23	100.00

No. 213.—*Pocketknives:* United States; 1897-98; unit, 1 dozen.
Ivory handle; Congress pattern; 3¼ inches long; ¼-inch German-silver bolsters; brass lined; 2 blades of forged English Wardlow steel.

	Amount.	Per cent of total.
Cost of labor in transforming materials	$1.89	57.80
Cost of materials and all other items except labor	1.38	42.20
Total cost	3.27	100.00

No. 214.—*Pocketknives:* United States; 1897-98; unit, 1 dozen.
Of the same general description as product No. 213, but having 4 blades.

	Amount.	Per cent of total.
Cost of labor in transforming materials	$2.53	57.24
Cost of materials and all other items except labor	1.89	42.76
Total cost	4.42	100.00

No. 215.—*Pocketknives:* United States; 1897; unit, 1 dozen.
Stag handle; Senator pattern; 3⅝ inches long; medium German-silver bolsters; brass lined; 2 blades of English Wardlow steel.

	Amount.	Per cent of total.
Cost of labor in transforming materials	$2.56	83.12
Cost of materials and all other items except labor	.52	16.88
Total cost	3.08	100.00

No. 216.—*Pocketknives:* United States; 1897; unit, 1 dozen.
Of the same general description as product No. 215, but having 4 blades.

	Amount.	Per cent of total.
Cost of labor in transforming materials	$4.25	86.21
Cost of materials and all other items except labor	.68	13.79
Total cost	4.93	100.00

No. 217.—*Pocketknives:* United States; 1897; unit, 1 dozen.
Stag handle; Congress pattern; 3¼ inches long; ⅜-inch iron bolsters; iron lined; 2 blades of Thos. Firths & Sons' English blade steel.

	Amount.	Per cent of total.
Cost of labor in transforming materials	$1.93	66.78
Cost of materials and all other items except labor	.96	33.22
Total cost	2.89	100.00

No. 218.—*Pocketknives:* United States; 1897; unit, 1 dozen.
Of the same general description as product No. 217, but having 4 blades.

	Amount.	Per cent of total.
Cost of labor in transforming materials	$3.21	70.09
Cost of materials and all other items except labor	1.37	29.91
Total cost	4.58	100.00

No. 219.—*Pocketknives:* United States; 1897–98; unit, 1 dozen.
Stag handle; Congress pattern; 3½ inches long; ½-inch iron bolsters; iron lined; 2 blades of forged English Wardlow steel.

	Amount.	Per cent of total.
Cost of labor in transforming materials	$1.67	60.07
Cost of materials and all other items except labor	1.11	39.93
Total cost	2.78	100.00

No. 220.—*Pocketknives:* United States; 1897–98; unit, 1 dozen.
Of the same general description as product No. 219, but having 4 blades.

	Amount.	Per cent of total.
Cost of labor in transforming materials	$2.89	65.38
Cost of materials and all other items except labor	1.53	34.62
Total cost	4.42	100.00

No. 221.—*Pocketknives:* United States; 1897–98; unit, 1 dozen.
Stag handle; bolster pattern; 3¼ inches long; ½-inch German-silver bolsters; brass lined; 3 blades of forged English Wardlow steel.

	Amount.	Per cent of total.
Cost of labor in transforming materials	$1.79	53.92
Cost of materials and all other items except labor	1.53	46.08
Total cost	3.32	100.00

No. 222.—*Pocketknives:* United States; 1897; unit, 1 dozen.
Ebony handle; Senator pattern; 3½ inches long; ¼-inch German-silver bolsters; brass lined; 2 blades of Thos. Firths & Sons' English blade steel.

	Amount.	Per cent of total.
Cost of labor in transforming materials	$2.10	69.08
Cost of materials and all other items except labor	.94	30.92
Total cost	3.04	100.00

No. 223.—*Pocketknives:* United States; 1897; unit, 1 dozen.
Of the same general description as product No. 222, but having 3 blades.

	Amount.	Per cent of total.
Cost of labor in transforming materials	$3.13	71.46
Cost of materials and all other items except labor	1.25	28.54
Total cost	4.38	100.00

No. 224.—*Pocketknives:* United States; 1897-98; unit, 1 dozen.
Ebony handle; bolster pattern; 3½ inches long; ⅛-inch German silver bolsters; brass lined; 3 blades of forged English Wardlow steel.

	Amount.	Per cent of total.
Cost of labor in transforming materials	$1.74	59.79
Cost of materials and all other items except labor	1.17	40.21
Total cost	2.91	100.00

No. 225.—*Pocketknives:* United States; 1897-98; unit, 1 dozen.
Ebony handle; 3½ inches long; ⅛-inch German silver bolster on one end; brass lined; 2 blades of forged English Wardlow steel.

	Amount.	Per cent of total.
Cost of labor in transforming materials	$1.54	59.46
Cost of materials and all other items except labor	1.05	40.54
Total cost	2.59	100.00

No. 226.—*Pocketknives:* United States; 1897-98; unit, 1 dozen.
Of the same general description as product No. 225, but having lighter handle and blades.

	Amount.	Per cent of total.
Cost of labor in transforming materials	$1.44	60.25
Cost of materials and all other items except labor	.95	39.75
Total cost	2.39	100.00

No. 227.—*Pocketknives:* United States; 1897; unit, 1 dozen.
Ebony handle; jackknife; 3⅝ inches long; medium German silver bolsters; brass lined; 2 blades of best English steel.

	Amount.	Per cent of total.
Cost of labor in transforming materials	$1.89	77.78
Cost of materials and all other items except labor	.54	22.22
Total cost	2.43	100.00

No. 228.—*Pocketknives:* United States; 1897; unit, 1 dozen.
Of the same general description as product No. 227, but 3⅞ inches long.

	Amount.	Per cent of total.
Cost of labor in transforming materials	$2.11	73.01
Cost of materials and all other items except labor	.78	26.99
Total cost	2.89	100.00

No. 229.—*Pocketknives:* United States; 1897; unit, 1 dozen.
Of the same general description as product No. 227, but 3¾ inches long, and having 3 blades.

	Amount.	Per cent of total.
Cost of labor in transforming materials	$2.54	72.99
Cost of materials and all other items except labor	.94	27.01
Total cost	3.48	100.00

No. 230.—*Pocketknives:* United States; 1897; unit, 1 dozen.
Ebony handle; straight jackknife; 3¼ inches long; medium iron bolster; iron lined; 2 blades of English Wardlow steel.

	Amount.	Per cent of total.
Cost of labor in transforming materials	$1.79	81.36
Cost of materials and all other items except labor	.41	18.64
Total cost	2.20	100.00

No. 231.—*Pocketknives:* United States; 1897; unit, 1 dozen.
Redwood handle; jackknife; 3¼ inches long; ½-inch German silver bolster on one end; brass lined; 2 blades of Thos. Firths & Sons' English blade steel.

	Amount.	Per cent of total.
Cost of labor in transforming materials	$1.43	62.72
Cost of materials and all other items except labor	.85	37.28
Total cost	2.28	100.00

No. 232.—*Pocketknives:* United States; 1897; unit, 1 dozen.
Of the same general description as product No. 231, but 3½ inches long.

	Amount.	Per cent of total.
Cost of labor in transforming materials	$1.54	61.35
Cost of materials and all other items except labor	.97	38.65
Total cost	2.51	100.00

No. 233.—*Pocketknives:* United States; 1897; unit, 1 dozen.
Of the same general description as product No. 231, but 3¾ inches long.

	Amount.	Per cent of total.
Cost of labor in transforming materials	$1.71	60.21
Cost of materials and all other items except labor	1.13	39.79
Total cost	2.84	100.00

No. 234.—*Pocketknives:* United States; 1897; unit, 1 dozen.

Of the same general description as product No. 231, but with iron bolster and iron lined.

	Amount.	Per cent of total.
Cost of labor in transforming materials	$1.18	65.92
Cost of materials and all other items except labor	.61	34.08
Total cost	1.79	100.00

No. 235.—*Pocketknives:* United States; 1897-98; unit, 1 dozen.

Redwood handle; jackknife; 3¾ inches long; ½-inch iron bolster on one end; iron lined; 2 blades of forged English Wardlow steel.

	Amount.	Per cent of total.
Cost of labor in transforming materials	$1.75	61.84
Cost of materials and all other items except labor	1.08	38.16
Total cost	2.83	100.00

No. 236.—*Pocketknives:* United States; 1897-98; unit, 1 dozen.

Redwood handle; jackknife; 3¼ inches long; ½-inch iron bolsters; iron lined; 2 blades of forged English Wardlow steel.

	Amount.	Per cent of total.
Cost of labor in transforming materials	$0.89	50.57
Cost of materials and all other items except labor	.87	49.43
Total cost	1.76	100.00

No. 237.—*Pocketknives:* United States; 1897; unit, 1 dozen.

Redwood handle; straight jackknife; 3¼ inches long; medium iron bolster; iron lined; 2 blades of English Wardlow steel.

	Amount.	Per cent of total.
Cost of labor in transforming materials	$1.37	83.03
Cost of materials and all other items except labor	.28	16.97
Total cost	1.65	100.00

No. 238.—*Pocketknives:* Great Britain; 1897; unit, 1 dozen.

Ivory handle; average size; metal bolsters and shield; 2 blades of good quality steel.

	Amount.	Per cent of total.
Cost of labor in transforming materials	$1.38	87.34
Cost of materials and all other items except labor	.20	12.66
Total cost	1.58	100.00

No. 239.—*Table knives:* United States; 1897-98; unit, 1 dozen.

Pearl handle, 3¾ inches long; sterling silver ferrule, ¾ inch long; flush plain bolster; blade, 5¾ to 6 inches long; drawn and forged of fine grade American crucible steel.

	mount.	Per cent of total.
Cost of labor in transforming materials	$3.22	36.59
Cost of materials and all other items except labor	5.58	63.41
Total cost	8.80	100.00

No. 240.—*Table knives:* United States; 1897-98; unit, 1 dozen.

Pearl handle, 2⅝ inches long; sterling silver ferrule, 1 inch long; ¼ inch flush bolster; blade, 5¼ to 5¾ inches long; drawn and forged of fine grade American crucible steel and silver plated.

	Amount.	Per cent of total.
Cost of labor in transforming materials	$2.40	22.43
Cost of materials and all other items except labor	8.30	77.57
Total cost	10.70	100.00

No. 241.—*Table knives:* United States; 1897-98; unit, 1 dozen.

Pearl handle, 2¾ inches long; sterling silver ferrule, ⅞ inch long; plain ¼-inch bolster; blade, 5¼ to 6¼ inches long; forged of high grade American crucible steel and silver plated.

	Amount.	Per cent of total.
Cost of labor in transforming materials	$2.28	23.90
Cost of materials and all other items except labor	7.26	76.10
Total cost	9.54	100.00

No. 242.—*Table knives:* United States; 1897-98; unit, 1 dozen.

Ivory handle of best grade, 3½ inches long; plain ½-inch bolster; blade, 5¾ to 6 inches long; drawn and forged of fine grade American crucible steel.

	Amount.	Per cent of total.
Cost of labor in transforming materials	$2.035	33.31
Cost of materials and all other items except labor	4.075	66.69
Total cost	6.11	100.00

No. 243.—*Table knives:* United States; 1897-98; unit, 1 dozen.

Of the same general description as product No. 242, but second quality of ivory is used in the handle.

	Amount.	Per cent of total.
Cost of labor in transforming materials	$2.035	36.67
Cost of materials and all other items except labor	3.515	63.33
Total cost	5.55	100.00

No. 244.—*Table knives:* United States; 1897-98; unit, 1 dozen.
Of the same general description as product No. 242, but third quality of ivory is used in the handle.

	Amount.	Per cent of total.
Cost of labor in transforming materials	$2.035	41.03
Cost of materials and all other items except labor	2.925	58.97
Total cost	4.96	100.00

No. 245.—*Table knives:* United States; 1897-98; unit, 1 dozen.
Ivory handle of medium grade, 3¾ inches long; plain ½-inch bolster; blade, 5¼ to 6¼ inches long; drawn and forged of ordinary grade American crucible steel.

	Amount.	Per cent of total.
Cost of labor in transforming materials	$1.30	21.52
Cost of materials and all other items except labor	4.74	78.48
Total cost	6.04	100.00

No. 246.—*Table knives:* United States; 1897-98; unit, 1 dozen.
Ivory handle of best grade, 3½ inches long; plain ½-inch bolster; blade, 5¼ to 6¼ inches long; forged of fine grade American crucible steel.

	Amount.	Per cent of total.
Cost of labor in transforming materials	$1.35	24.50
Cost of materials and all other items except labor	4.16	75.50
Total cost	5.51	100.00

No. 247.—*Table knives:* United States; 1897-98; unit, 1 dozen.
Of the same general description as product No. 246, but a lower grade of ivory is used in the handle.

	Amount.	Per cent of total.
Cost of labor in transforming materials	$1.35	28.54
Cost of materials and all other items except labor	3.38	71.46
Total cost	4.73	100.00

No. 248.—*Table knives:* United States; 1897-98; unit, 1 dozen.
Of the same general description as product No. 246, but a low grade of ivory is used in the handle.

	Amount.	Per cent of total.
Cost of labor in transforming materials	$1.35	45.92
Cost of materials and all other items except labor	1.59	54.08
Total cost	2.94	100.00

No. 249.—*Table knives:* United States; 1897; unit, 1 dozen.
Ivory handle, 4 inches long; ½-inch bolster; blade, 6 inches long, of best English steel.

	Amount.	Per cent of total.
Cost of labor in transforming materials	$0.94	11.58
Cost of materials and all other items except labor	7.18	88.42
Total cost	8.12	100.00

No. 250.—*Table knives:* United States; 1897-98; unit, 1 dozen.

Celluloid handle, 3½ inches long; plain ½-inch bolster; blade, 5¾ to 6 inches long; drawn and forged of fine grade American crucible steel.

	Amount.	Per cent of total.
Cost of labor in transforming materials	$1.555	55.34
Cost of materials and all other items except labor	1.255	44.66
Total cost	2.81	100.00

No. 251.—*Table knives:* United States; 1897-98; unit, 1 dozen.

Celluloid handle, 4 inches long; plain ½-inch bolster; blade, 5½ to 6 inches long; drawn and forged of ordinary grade American crucible steel.

	Amount.	Per cent of total.
Cost of labor in transforming materials	$1.02	50.50
Cost of materials and all other items except labor	1.00	49.50
Total cost	2.02	100.00

No. 252.—*Table knives:* United States; 1897-98; unit, 1 dozen.

Celluloid handle, 3¾ inches long; plain ½-inch bolster; blade, 5¼ to 6¼ inches long; forged of high grade American crucible steel.

	Amount.	Per cent of total.
Cost of labor in transforming materials	$1.28	47.23
Cost of materials and all other items except labor	1.43	52.77
Total cost	2.71	100.00

No. 253.—*Table knives:* United States; 1897; unit, 1 dozen.

Celluloid handle, 3½ inches long; ½-inch bolster; blade, 6 inches long, of best English steel.

	Amount.	Per cent of total.
Cost of labor in transforming materials	$0.77	38.12
Cost of materials and all other items except labor	1.25	61.88
Total cost	2.02	100.00

No. 254.—*Table knives:* United States; 1897-98; unit, 1 dozen.

Rubber handle, 3½ inches long; plain ½-inch bolster; blade, 5¾ to 6 inches long, drawn and forged, of fine grade American crucible steel.

	Amount.	Per cent of total.
Cost of labor in transforming materials	$1.395	71.54
Cost of materials and all other items except labor	.555	28.46
Total cost	1.95	100.00

No. 255.—*Table knives:* United States; 1897-98; unit, 1 dozen.

Rubber handle, 4 inches long; plain ½-inch bolster; blade, 5½ to 6 inches long, drawn and forged, of ordinary grade American crucible steel.

	Amount.	Per cent of total.
Cost of labor in transforming materials	$1.02	54.26
Cost of materials and all other items except labor	.86	45.74
Total cost	1.88	100.00

No. 256.—*Table knives:* United States; 1897; unit, 1 dozen.
Rubber handle, 3½ inches long; ½-inch bolster; blade, 6 inches long, of best English steel.

	Amount.	Per cent of total.
Cost of labor in transforming materials	$0.75	43.35
Cost of materials and all other items except labor	.98	56.65
Total cost	1.73	100.00

No. 257.—*Table knives:* United States; 1897–98; unit, 1 dozen.
White bone handle, 3½ inches long; ¼-inch metal bolster; blade, 5¼ inches long, machine made and ground, of cheap open-hearth steel.

	Amount.	Per cent of total.
Cost of labor in transforming materials	$0.4317	66.16
Cost of materials and all other items except labor	.2208	33.84
Total cost	.6525	100.00

No. 258.—*Table knives:* United States; 1897–98; unit, 1 dozen.
White bone handle, 3⅜ inches long; plain ½-inch bolster; blade, 5½ to 6 inches long, drawn and forged, of best open-hearth steel.

	Amount.	Per cent of total.
Cost of labor in transforming materials	$0.87	56.13
Cost of materials and all other items except labor	.68	43.87
Total cost	1.55	100.00

No. 259.—*Table knives:* United States; 1897–98; unit, 1 dozen.
White bone handle, 3½ inches long; plain ½-inch bolster; blade, 5¾ to 6¼ inches long; forged, of high-grade American crucible steel.

	Amount.	Per cent of total.
Cost of labor in transforming materials	$1.28	72.73
Cost of materials and all other items except labor	.48	27.27
Total cost	1.76	100.00

No. 260.—*Table knives:* United States; 1897–98; unit, 1 dozen.
Redwood handle, 3½ inches long; no bolster; blade, 5¼ inches long, machine made and ground, of cheap open-hearth steel.

	Amount.	Per cent of total.
Cost of labor in transforming materials	$0.2883	77.92
Cost of materials and all other items except labor	.0817	22.08
Total cost	.37	100.00

No. 261.—*Table knives:* United States; 1897–98; unit, 1 dozen.
Of the same general description as product No. 260, but having ¼-inch metal bolster.

	Amount.	Per cent of total.
Cost of labor in transforming materials	$0.3383	75.46
Cost of materials and all other items except labor	.11	24.54
Total cost	.4483	100.00

No. 262.—*Table knives:* United States; 1897–98; unit, 1 dozen.

Redwood or cocobolo handle, 3½ inches long; no bolster; blade, 5⅞ inches long, machine cut, of low-grade open-hearth steel.

	Amount.	Per cent of total.
Cost of labor in transforming materials	$0.162	64.29
Cost of materials and all other items except labor	.09	35.71
Total cost	.252	100.00

No. 263.—*Table knives:* United States; 1897–98; unit, 1 dozen.

Redwood or cocobolo handle, 3½ inches long; plain ¼-inch bolster; blade, 6 inches long, machine cut, of low-grade open-hearth steel, curved, and of slightly better finish than in product No. 262.

	Amount.	Per cent of total.
Cost of labor in transforming materials	$0.223	64.08
Cost of materials and all other items except labor	.125	35.92
Total cost	.348	100.00

No. 264.—*Table knives:* United States; 1897–98; unit, 1 dozen.

Redwood handle, 3½ inches long; no bolster; blade, 5¼ inches long, forged, of cheap grade American crucible steel.

	Amount.	Per cent of total.
Cost of labor in transforming materials	$0.21	63.18
Cost of materials and all other items except labor	.1224	36.82
Total cost	.3324	100.00

No. 265.—*Table knives:* United States; 1897–98; unit, 1 dozen.

Solid steel; handle and blade in one piece; handle, 3¼ inches long; plain ½-inch bolster; blade, 5½ inches long, drawn and forged, of best grade open-hearth steel.

	Amount.	Per cent of total.
Cost of labor in transforming materials	$0.415	58.62
Cost of materials and all other items except labor	.293	41.38
Total cost	.708	100.00

No. 266.—*Table knives:* United States; 1897–98; unit, 1 dozen.

Solid steel; handle and blade in one piece; handle, 3¾ inches long; blade, 5¼ to 6 inches long, forged, of cheap grade American crucible steel.

	Amount.	Per cent of total.
Cost of labor in transforming materials	$0.88	79.28
Cost of materials and all other items except labor	.23	20.72
Total cost	1.11	100.00

No. 267.—*Table knives:* United States; 1897; unit, 1 dozen.

Solid steel; handle and blade in one piece; handle, 3¾ inches long; ½-inch bolster; blade, 5½ inches long; of best English steel.

	Amount.	Per cent of total.
Cost of labor in transforming materials	$0.51	53.68
Cost of materials and all other items except labor	.44	46.32
Total cost	.95	100.00

No. 268.—*Table knives:* Belgium; 1897; unit, 1 dozen.

Ebony handle; medium length; blade, of Siemens refined bar steel; an ordinary restaurant knife; handle bought already formed.

	Amount.	Per cent of total.
Cost of labor in transforming materials	$0.386	33.33
Cost of materials and all other items except labor	.772	66.67
Total cost	1.158	100.00

No. 269.—*Table knives:* Great Britain; 1897; unit, 1 dozen.

Ivory handle, 4 inches long; ½-inch bolster; blade, 6¼ inches long, machine made, of good ordinary steel.

	Amount.	Per cent of total.
Cost of labor in transforming materials	$0.85	18.89
Cost of materials and all other items except labor	3.65	81.11
Total cost	4.50	100.00

No. 270.—*Table knives:* Great Britain; 1897; unit, 1 dozen.

Of the same general description as product No. 269, but having hand-made blade.

	Amount.	Per cent of total.
Cost of labor in transforming materials	$0.91	19.96
Cost of materials and all other items except labor	3.65	80.04
Total cost	4.56	100.00

No. 271.—*Table-knife blades:* United States; 1897-98; unit, 1 dozen.

5¾ to 6 inches long; drawn and forged of fine grade American crucible steel; used in product No. 242.

	Amount.	Per cent of total.
Cost of labor in transforming materials	$0.70	80.00
Cost of materials and all other items except labor	.175	20.00
Total cost	.875	100.00

No. 272.—*Table-knife blades:* United States; 1897-98; unit, 1 dozen.

5¼ to 5¾ inches long; drawn and forged of fine grade American crucible steel; used in product No. 240.

	Amount.	Per cent of total.
Cost of labor in transforming materials	$0.62	65.96
Cost of materials and all other items except labor	.32	34.04
Total cost	.94	100.00

No. 273.—*Table-knife blades:* United States; 1897-98; unit, 1 dozen.

5¼ to 6¼ inches long; forged of fine grade American crucible steel; used in product No. 246.

	Amount.	Per cent of total.
Cost of labor in transforming materials	$1.02	79.69
Cost of materials and all other items except labor	.26	20.31
Total cost	1.28	100.00

No. 274.—*Table-knife blades:* United States; 1897; unit, 1 dozen.
6 inches long; of best English steel; used in product No. 249.

	Amount.	Per cent of total.
Cost of labor in transforming materials	$0.63	53.39
Cost of materials and all other items except labor	.55	46.61
Total cost	1.18	100.00

No. 275.—*Table-knife blades:* United States; 1897; unit, 1 dozen.
6 inches long; of best English steel; used in product No. 253.

	Amount.	Per cent of total.
Cost of labor in transforming materials	$0.55	51.89
Cost of materials and all other items except labor	.51	48.11
Total cost	1.06	100.00

No. 276.—*Table-knife blades:* United States; 1897–98; unit, 1 dozen.
5½ to 6 inches long; drawn and forged of best grade open-hearth steel; used in product No. 258.

	Amount.	Per cent of total.
Cost of labor in transforming materials	$0.48	68.57
Cost of materials and all other items except labor	.22	31.43
Total cost	.70	100.00

No. 277.—*Table-knife blades:* United States; 1897–98; unit, 1 dozen.
5½ to 6½ inches long; drawn and forged of ordinary grade American crucible steel; used in product No. 245.

	Amount.	Per cent of total.
Cost of labor in transforming materials	$0.60	71.43
Cost of materials and all other items except labor	.24	28.57
Total cost	.84	100.00

No. 278.—*Table-knife blades:* United States; 1897–98; unit, 1 dozen.
5½ to 6 inches long; drawn and forged of ordinary grade American crucible steel; used in product No. 251.

	Amount.	Per cent of total.
Cost of labor in transforming materials	$0.57	71.25
Cost of materials and all other items except labor	.23	28.75
Total cost	.80	100.00

No. 279.—*Table-knife blades:* United States; 1897–98; unit, 1 dozen.
5¼ inches long; forged of cheap grade American crucible steel; used in product No. 264.

	Amount.	Per cent of total.
Cost of labor in transforming materials	$0.179	70.75
Cost of materials and all other items except labor	.074	29.25
Total cost	.253	100.00

No. 280.—*Table-knife blades:* United States; 1897-98; unit, 1 dozen.
5¼ inches long; machine made and ground; of cheap open-hearth steel; used in product No. 260.

	Amount.	Per cent of total.
Cost of labor in transforming materials	$0.1942	85.36
Cost of materials and all other items except labor	.0333	14.64
Total cost	.2275	100.00

No. 281.—*Table-knife blades:* United States; 1897-98; unit, 1 dozen.
5¾ inches long; machine cut; of low grade open-hearth steel; used in product No. 262.

	Amount.	Per cent of total.
Cost of labor in transforming materials	$0.078	50.00
Cost of materials and all other items except labor	.078	50.00
Total cost	.156	100.00

No. 282.—*Table-knife blades:* United States; 1897-98; unit, 1 dozen.
6 inches long; machine cut; of low-grade open-hearth steel; curved; of slightly better finish than product No. 281; used in product No. 263.

	Amount.	Per cent of total.
Cost of labor in transforming materials	$0.0912	50.33
Cost of materials and all other items except labor	.0900	49.67
Total cost	.1812	100.00

No. 283.—*Table-knife blades:* Belgium; 1897; unit, 1 dozen.
Medium size; of Siemens refined bar steel; used in product No. 268.

	Amount.	Per cent of total.
Cost of labor in transforming materials	$0.3860	80.00
Cost of materials and all other items except labor	.0965	20.00
Total cost	.4825	100.00

No. 284.—*Table-knife blades:* Great Britain; 1897; unit, 1 dozen.
6½ inches long; machine made; of good ordinary steel; used in product No. 269.

	Amount.	Per cent of total.
Cost of labor in transforming materials	$0.4461	52.38
Cost of materials and all other items except labor	.4055	47.62
Total cost	.8516	100.00

No. 285.—*Table-knife blades:* Great Britain; 1897; unit, 1 dozen.
6½ inches long; hand made; of good ordinary steel; used in product No. 270.

	Amount.	Per cent of total.
Cost of labor in transforming materials	$0.5070	55.56
Cost of materials and all other items except labor	.4055	44.44
Total cost	.9125	100.00

FURNITURE.

No. 286.—*Plain tables:* United States; 1897; unit, 1 table.
Oak; turned legs, 3 inches in diameter; size of top, 24x42 inches.

	Amount.	Per cent of total.
Cost of labor in transforming materials	$0.70	42.17
Cost of materials and all other items except labor	.96	57.83
Total cost	1.66	100.00

No. 287.—*Plain tables:* United States; 1898; unit, 1 table.
Oak; turned legs, 3 inches in diameter; size of top, 32x40 inches; made in lots of 100 or more.

	Amount.	Per cent of total.
Cost of labor in transforming materials	$0.63	36.63
Cost of materials and all other items except labor	1.09	63.37
Total cost	1.72	100.00

No. 288.—*Plain tables:* United States; 1897-98; unit, 1 table.
Oak; turned legs, 3 inches in diameter; size of top, 30x40 inches; made in lots of 100 or more.

	Amount.	Per cent of total.
Cost of labor in transforming materials	$0.49	29.88
Cost of materials and all other items except labor	1.15	70.12
Total cost	1.64	100.00

No. 289.—*Plain tables:* United States; 1897; unit, 1 table.
Poplar top and rails; maple legs, turned, 3 inches in diameter; size of top, 24x42 inches.

	Amount.	Per cent of total.
Cost of labor in transforming materials	$0.50	43.10
Cost of materials and all other items except labor	.66	56.90
Total cost	1.16	100.00

No. 290.—*Plain tables:* Great Britain; 1897; unit, 1 table.
Oak; turned legs, 4 inches in diameter; size of top, 42x42 inches.

	Amount.	Per cent of total.
Cost of labor in transforming materials	$1.14	31.06
Cost of materials and all other items except labor	2.53	68.94
Total cost	3.67	100.00

No. 291.—*Dining tables:* United States; 1897; unit, 1 table.
Oak; extension top; turned legs, 3½ inches in diameter; size of top, 6 feet 6 inches long and 3 feet 6 inches wide.

	Amount.	Per cent of total.
Cost of labor in transforming materials	$1.76	44.11
Cost of materials and all other items except labor	2.23	55.89
Total cost	3.99	100.00

No. 292.—*Dining tables:* United States; 1898; unit, 1 table.
Oak; extension top; turned legs, 3 inches in diameter; size of top, 6 feet 6 inches long and 3 feet 6 inches wide; made in lots of 100 or more.

	Amount.	Per cent of total.
Cost of labor in transforming materials	$0.81	37.85
Cost of materials and all other items except labor	1.33	62.15
Total cost	2.14	100.00

No. 293.—*Dining tables:* United States; 1897-98; unit, 1 table.
Oak; extension top; turned legs, 3 inches in diameter; size of top, 6 feet 6 inches long and 3 feet 6 inches wide; made in lots of 100 or more.

	Amount.	Per cent of total.
Cost of labor in transforming materials	$0.675	25.67
Cost of materials and all other items except labor	1.955	74.33
Total cost	2.63	100.00

No. 294.—*Dining tables:* Great Britain; 1897; unit, 1 table.
Oak; extension top; turned legs, 4 inches in diameter; size of top, 6 feet 6 inches long and 3 feet 6 inches wide.

	Amount.	Per cent of total.
Cost of labor in transforming materials	$2.66	39.88
Cost of materials and all other items except labor	4.01	60.12
Total cost	6.67	100.00

No. 295.—*Bentwood dining chairs:* United States; 1897; unit, 1 dozen.
Plain; varnished; without arms; caned seat.

	Amount.	Per cent of total.
Cost of labor in transforming materials *a*	$3.85	45.29
Cost of materials and all other items except labor	4.65	54.71
Total cost	8.50	100.00

a A large proportion of convict labor is employed in the production of these chairs.

No. 296.—*Bentwood dining chairs:* United States; 1897-98; unit, 1 dozen.
Plain; varnished; without arms; caned seat.

	Amount.	Per cent of total.
Cost of labor in transforming materials	$2.82	33.02
Cost of materials and all other items except labor	5.72	66.98
Total cost	8.54	100.00

No. 297.—*Bentwood library chairs:* United States; 1897; unit, 1 dozen.
Plain; varnished; with arms; caned seat; larger and heavier than product No. 295.

	Amount.	Per cent of total.
Cost of labor in transforming materials *a*	$6.25	50.00
Cost of materials and all other items except labor	6.25	50.00
Total cost	12.50	100.00

a A large proportion of convict labor is employed in the production of these chairs.

No. 298.—*Bentwood library chairs:* United States; 1897-98; unit, 1 dozen.
Plain; varnished; with arms; caned seat: larger and heavier than product No. 296.

	Amount.	Per cent of total.
Cost of labor in transforming materials	$4.62	37.50
Cost of materials and all other items except labor	7.70	62.50
Total cost	12.32	100.00

No. 299.—*Bentwood dining chairs:* Belgium; 1897; unit, 1 dozen.
Plain; varnished; without arms; caned seat.

	Amount.	Per cent of total.
Cost of labor in transforming materials	$4.63	50.00
Cost of materials and all other items except labor	4.63	50.00
Total cost	9.26	100.00

GLASS.

No. 300.—*Green glass pickle bottles:* United States; 1897; unit, 1 gross.
Crosse & Blackwell style; holding 20 ounces, and weighing 16½ ounces per bottle

	Amount.	Per cent of total.
Cost of labor in transforming materials	$1.63	41.48
Cost of materials and all other items except labor	2.30	58.52
Total cost	3.93	100.00

No. 301.—*Green glass pickle bottles:* United States; 1897; unit, 1 gross.
Crosse & Blackwell style; holding 20 ounces, and weighing 16 ounces per bottle.

	Amount.	Per cent of total.
Cost of labor in transforming materials	$1.605	54.04
Cost of materials and all other items except labor	1.365	45.96
Total cost	2.97	100.00

No. 302.—*Green glass pickle bottles:* United States; 1897; unit, 1 gross.
Crosse & Blackwell style; holding 20 ounces, and weighing 16 ounces per bottle.

	Amount.	Per cent of total.
Cost of labor in transforming materials	$1.60	52.63
Cost of materials and all other items except labor	1.44	47.37
Total cost	3.04	100.00

No. 303.—*Green glass pickle bottles:* United States; 1898; unit, 1 gross.
Holding 20 ounces, and weighing 17 ounces per bottle.

	Amount.	Per cent of total.
Cost of labor in transforming materials	$1.88	60.06
Cost of materials and all other items except labor	1.25	39.94
Total cost	3.13	100.00

No. 304.—*Green glass pickle bottles:* Great Britain; 1897; unit, 1 gross.
Crosse & Blackwell style; holding 20 ounces, and weighing 16 to 17 ounces per bottle.

	Amount.	Per cent of total.
Cost of labor in transforming materials	$1.03	41.37
Cost of materials and all other items except labor	1.46	58.63
Total cost	2.49	100.00

No. 305.—*Green glass spirit bottles:* United States; 1897; unit, 1 gross.
Holding 26⅔ ounces, and weighing 25 ounces per bottle.

	Amount.	Per cent of total.
Cost of labor in transforming materials	$1.97	36.08
Cost of materials and all other items except labor	3.49	63.92
Total cost	5.46	100.00

No. 306.—*Green glass spirit bottles:* United States; 1897; unit, 1 gross.
Holding 26⅔ ounces, and weighing 25 ounces per bottle.

	Amount.	Per cent of total.
Cost of labor in transforming materials	$1.88	45.52
Cost of materials and all other items except labor	2.25	54.48
Total cost	4.13	100.00

No. 307.—*Green glass spirit bottles:* United States; 1898; unit, 1 gross.
Holding 26 ounces, and weighing 26 ounces per bottle.

	Amount.	Per cent of total.
Cost of labor in transforming materials	$2.26	60.27
Cost of materials and all other items except labor	1.49	39.73
Total cost	3.75	100.00

No. 308.—*Green glass spirit bottles:* Great Britain; 1897; unit, 1 gross.
Holding 26⅔ ounces, and weighing 25 ounces per bottle.

	Amount.	Per cent of total.
Cost of labor in transforming materials	$1.15	37.58
Cost of materials and all other items except labor	1.91	62.42
Total cost	3.06	100.00

MEN'S HATS.

No. 309.—*Stiff fur hats:* United States; 1897-98; unit, 1 dozen.
Cheap grade; made of coney fur; crown, 5¼ inches deep; brim, 2 inches wide; unlined; bound edge; union band, 2 inches wide.

	Amount.	Per cent of total.
Cost of labor in transforming materials	$5.535	53.48
Cost of materials and all other items except labor	4.815	46.52
Total cost	10.35	100.00

No. 310.—*Stiff fur hats:* United States; 1897-98; unit, 1 dozen.
Medium grade; made of coney fur; crown, 5¼ inches deep; brim, 2 inches wide; unlined; bound edge; union band, 2 inches wide.

	Amount.	Per cent of total.
Cost of labor in transforming materials	$6.77	50.15
Cost of materials and all other items except labor	6.73	49.85
Total cost	13.50	100.00

No. 311.—*Stiff fur hats:* United States; 1897-98; unit, 1 dozen.
Fine grade; made of coney fur; crown, 5¼ inches deep; brim, 2 inches wide; unlined; bound edge; silk band, 1 inch wide.

	Amount.	Per cent of total.
Cost of labor in transforming materials	$8.015	45.77
Cost of materials and all other items except labor	9.495	54.23
Total cost	17.51	100.00

No. 312.—*Stiff fur hats:* United States; 1897-98; unit, 1 dozen.
Medium grade; made of mixed fur; crown, 5½ inches deep; brim, 2⅛ inches wide; unlined; bound edge; union band, 1 inch wide.

	Amount.	Per cent of total.
Cost of labor in transforming materials	$8.25	55.93
Cost of materials and all other items except labor	6.50	44.07
Total cost	14.75	100.00

No. 313.—*Stiff fur hats:* United States; 1897-98; unit, 1 dozen.
Of the same general description as product No. 312, but having silk binding and band, finer trimmings, and made of finer fur.

	Amount.	Per cent of total.
Cost of labor in transforming materials	$9.60	48.48
Cost of materials and all other items except labor	10.20	51.52
Total cost	19.80	100.00

No. 314.—*Stiff fur hats:* United States; 1897-98; unit, 1 dozen.
Of the same general description as product 312, but having silk binding and band, extra fine quality of trimmings, and made of extra fine quality of fur.

	Amount.	Per cent of total.
Cost of labor in transforming materials	$10.60	48.51
Cost of materials and all other items except labor	11.25	51.49
Total cost	21.85	100.00

No. 315.—*Stiff fur hats:* United States; 1897-98; unit, 1 dozen.
Medium grade; made of mixed fur; crown, 5½ inches deep; brim, 2⅛ inches wide; unlined; bound edge; union band, 1 inch wide.

	Amount.	Per cent of total.
Cost of labor in transforming materials	$6.63	59.09
Cost of materials and all other items except labor	4.59	40.91
Total cost	11.22	100.00

No. 316.—*Stiff fur hats:* United States; 1897-98; unit, 1 dozen.
Of the same general description as product No. 315, but having finer trimmings, and made of finer fur.

	Amount.	Per cent of total.
Cost of labor in transforming materials	$9.84	55.62
Cost of materials and all other items except labor	7.85	44.38
Total cost	17.69	100.00

No. 317.—*Stiff fur hats:* Belgium; 1897; unit, 1 dozen.
Cheap grade; average size; poor quality of finishings.

	Amount.	Per cent of total.
Cost of labor in transforming materials	$3.13	38.59
Cost of materials and all other items except labor	4.98	61.41
Total cost	8.11	100.00

No. 318.—*Stiff fur hats:* Belgium; 1897; unit, 1 dozen.
Medium grade; average size; average quality of finishings.

	Amount.	Per cent of total.
Cost of labor in transforming materials	$3.474	30.00
Cost of materials and all other items except labor	8.106	70.00
Total cost	11.580	100.00

No. 319.—*Stiff fur hats:* Belgium; 1897; unit, 1 dozen.
Fine grade; average size; good quality of finishings.

	Amount.	Per cent of total.
Cost of labor in transforming materials	$4.93	26.61
Cost of materials and all other items except labor	13.60	73.39
Total cost	18.53	100.00

No. 320.—*Stiff fur hats:* Great Britain; 1897; unit, 1 dozen.
Medium grade; average size; average quality of finishings.

	Amount.	Per cent of total.
Cost of labor in transforming materials	$2.92 to $3.24	34.27 to 33.30
Cost of materials and all other items except labor	5.60 to 6.49	65.73 to 66.70
Total cost	8.52 to 9.73	100.00 100.00

No. 321.—*Stiff fur hats:* Great Britain; 1897; unit, 1 dozen.
Cheap grade; average size; poor quality of finishings.

	Amount.	Per cent of total.
Cost of labor in transforming materials	$2.92	48.03
Cost of materials and all other items except labor	3.16	51.97
Total cost	6.08	100.00

No. 322.—*Soft fur hats:* United States; 1897; unit, one dozen.
Cheap grade; made of rabbit fur; various shapes and sizes; unbound; unlined.

	Amount.	Per cent of total.
Cost of labor in transforming materials	$1.89	29.67
Cost of materials and all other items except labor	4.48	70.33
Total cost	6.37	100.00

No. 323.—*Soft fur hats:* United States; 1897-98; unit, 1 dozen.
Cheap grade; made of coney fur; crown, 6 inches deep; brim, 3 inches wide; unlined; bound edge; wide union band; tourist shape.

	Amount.	Per cent of total.
Cost of labor in transforming materials	$2.517	32.41
Cost of materials and all other items except labor	5.250	67.59
Total cost	7.767	100.00

No. 324.—*Soft fur hats:* United States; 1897-98; unit, 1 dozen.
Medium grade; made of coney fur; crown, 4½ inches deep if square, or 6 inches deep if round; brim, 3½ inches wide; unlined; unbound; narrow union band.

	Amount.	Per cent of total.
Cost of labor in transforming materials	$2.772	29.14
Cost of materials and all other items except labor	6.740	70.86
Total cost	9.512	100.00

No. 325.—*Soft fur hats:* United States; 1897-98; unit, 1 dozen.
Medium grade; made of coney fur; crown, 6 inches deep; brim, 4 inches wide; unlined; unbound; narrow union band.

	Amount.	Per cent of total.
Cost of labor in transforming materials	$3.027	26.94
Cost of materials and all other items except labor	8.210	73.06
Total cost	11.237	100.00

No. 326.—*Soft fur hats:* United States; 1897-98; unit, 1 dozen.
Medium grade; made of mixed fur; crown, 6 inches deep; brim, 3 inches wide; unlined; bound edge; union band, 2 inches wide.

	Amount.	Per cent of total.
Cost of labor in transforming materials	$5.43	41.01
Cost of materials and all other items except labor	7.81	58.99
Total cost	13.24	100.00

No. 327.—*Soft fur hats:* United States; 1897-98; unit, 1 dozen.
Of the same general description as product No. 326, but having finer trimmings and made of finer fur.

	Amount.	Per cent of total.
Cost of labor in transforming materials	$7.60	42.62
Cost of materials and all other items except labor	10.23	57.38
Total cost	17.83	100.00

No. 328.—*Soft fur hats:* Belgium; 1897; unit, 1 dozen.
Cheap grade; average size; average quality of finishings.

	Amount.	Per cent of total.
Cost of labor in transforming materials	$1.85	38.38
Cost of materials and all other items except labor	2.97	61.62
Total cost	4.82	100.00

No. 329.—*Soft fur hats:* Belgium; 1897; unit, 1 dozen.
Medium grade; average size; average quality of finishings.

	Amount.	Per cent of total.
Cost of labor in transforming materials	$3.474	30.00
Cost of materials and all other items except labor	8.106	70.00
Total cost	11.580	100.00

No. 330.—*Soft fur hats:* Belgium; 1897; unit, 1 dozen.
Fine grade; average size; good quality of finishings.

	Amount.	Per cent of total.
Cost of labor in transforming materials	$4.632	26.67
Cost of materials and all other items except labor	12.738	73.33
Total cost	17.370	100.00

No. 331.—*Soft fur hats:* Great Britain; 1897; unit, 1 dozen.
Medium grade; average size; average quality of finishings.

	Amount.	Per cent of total.
Cost of labor in transforming materials	$3.41 to $3.89	40.02 to 39.98
Cost of materials and all other items except labor	5.11 to 5.84	59.98 to 60.02
Total cost	8.52 to 9.73	100.00-100.00

No. 332.—*Soft wool hats:* United States; 1897; unit, 1 dozen.
Medium quality; crown 5½ inches deep; brim, 3¼ inches wide; lined; unbound.

	Amount.	Per cent of total.
Cost of labor in transforming materials	$0.82	20.35
Cost of materials and all other items except labor	3.21	79.65
Total cost	4.03	100.00

No. 333.—*Soft wool hats:* United States; 1897; unit, 1 dozen.
Medium quality; crown, 5½ inches deep; brim, 2¾ inches wide; unlined; bound edge.

	Amount.	Per cent of total.
Cost of labor in transforming materials	$0.78	25.91
Cost of materials and all other items except labor	2.23	74.09
Total cost	3.01	100.00

No. 334.—*Soft wool hats:* United States; 1897; unit, 1 dozen.
Crown, 5¼ inches deep; brim, 2¾ inches wide; unlined; bound edge; wide union band; fedora shape.

	Amount.	Per cent of total.
Cost of labor in transforming materials	$1.58	33.33
Cost of materials and all other items except labor	3.16	66.67
Total cost	4.74	100.00

No. 335.—*Soft wool hats:* United States; 1897; unit, 1 dozen.
Crown, 5 inches deep; brim, 2½ inches wide; unlined; unbound; narrow union band; crusher shape.

	Amount.	Per cent of total.
Cost of labor in transforming materials	$1.10	33.33
Cost of materials and all other items except labor	2.20	66.67
Total cost	3.30	100.00

No. 336.—*Soft wool hats:* United States; 1897; unit, 1 dozen.
Crown, 6 inches deep; brim, 3 inches wide; lined; raw edge; narrow union band.

	Amount.	Per cent of total.
Cost of labor in transforming materials	$1.05	23.70
Cost of materials and all other items except labor	3.38	76.30
Total cost	4.43	100.00

No. 337.—*Soft wool hats:* United States; 1897; unit, 1 dozen.
Crown, 5¾ inches deep; brim, 2¾ inches wide; unlined; unbound; welt edge; wide union band.

	Amount.	Per cent of total.
Cost of labor in transforming materials	$1.12	29.09
Cost of materials and all other items except labor	2.73	70.91
Total cost	3.85	100.00

No. 338.—*Soft wool hats:* United States; 1897; unit, 1 dozen.
Crown, 6 inches deep; brim, 3 inches wide; lined; bound edge; very wide union band; fedora shape.

	Amount.	Per cent of total.
Cost of labor in transforming materials	$1.26	23.64
Cost of materials and all other items except labor	4.07	76.36
Total cost	5.33	100.00

No. 339.—*Soft wool hats:* United States; 1897; unit, 1 dozen.
Unlined; raw edge; narrow union band; fedora shape.

	Amount.	Per cent of total.
Cost of labor in transforming materials	$1.02	28.18
Cost of materials and all other items except labor	2.60	71.82
Total cost	3.62	100.00

No. 340.—*Soft wool hats:* Great Britain; 1897; unit, 1 dozen.
Medium grade; average size; lined.

	Amount.	Per cent of total.
Cost of labor in transforming materials	$1.52	34.70
Cost of materials and all other items except labor	2.86	65.30
Total cost	4.38	100.00

No. 341.—*Soft wool hats:* Great Britain; 1897; unit, 1 dozen.
Medium grade; average size; unlined.

	Amount.	Per cent of total.
Cost of labor in transforming materials	$1.703	35.00
Cost of materials and all other items except labor	3.163	65.00
Total cost	4.866	100.00

No. 342.—*Flexible wool hats:* United States; 1897; unit, 1 dozen.
Medium grade; crown, 6 inches deep; brim, 2⅝ inches wide; unlined; bound edge; tourist or fedora shape.

	Amount.	Per cent of total.
Cost of labor in transforming materials	$0.90	25.57
Cost of materials and all other items except labor	2.62	74.43
Total cost	3.52	100.00

No. 343.—*Flexible wool hats:* Great Britain; 1897; unit, 1 dozen.
Medium grade; average size; unlined.

	Amount.	Per cent of total.
Cost of labor in transforming materials	$1.64	42.16
Cost of materials and all other items except labor	2.25	57.84
Total cost	3.89	100.00

IRON AND STEEL.

No. 344.—*Cast-iron pipe:* United States; 1897; unit, 1 ton (2,240 pounds).
Diameter, 6 inches; thickness, $\frac{7}{16}$ inch; weight, 30½ pounds per foot. [a]

	Amount.	Per cent of total.
Cost of labor in transforming materials	$4.22	23.23
Cost of materials and all other items except labor	13.95	76.77
Total cost	18.17	100.00

[a] This is the average size of cast-iron pipe produced by the establishment furnishing the information. Its cost represents the average cost of producing all sizes of cast-iron pipe from 3 inches to 48 inches in diameter.

No. 315.—*Cast-iron pipe:* United States; 1897; unit, 1 ton (2,240 pounds). Diameter, 4 inches; thickness, [illegible] inch; weight, 16½ pounds per foot.

	Amount.	Per cent of total.
Cost of labor in transforming materials	$5.22	27.23
Cost of materials and all other items except labor	13.95	72.77
Total cost	19.17	100.00

No. 316.—*Cast-iron pipe:* United States; 1897; unit, 1 ton (2,240 pounds). Diameter, 3 inches; thickness, [illegible] inch; weight, 11 pounds per foot.

	Amount.	Per cent of total.
Cost of labor in transforming materials	$6.22	30.84
Cost of materials and all other items except labor	13.95	69.16
Total cost	20.17	100.00

No. 317.—*Cast-iron pipe:* Great Britain; 1897; unit, 1 ton (2,240 pounds). Average of various sizes.

	Amount.	Per cent of total.
Cost of labor in transforming materials	$7.30	34.29
Cost of materials and all other items except labor	13.99	65.71
Total cost	21.29	100.00

No. 318.—*Basic pig iron:* United States; 1897–98; unit, 1 ton (2,240 pounds).

	Amount.	Per cent of total.
Cost of labor in transforming materials	$0.60	6.25
Cost of materials and all other items except labor	9.00	93.75
Total cost	9.60	100.00

No. 319.—*Bessemer pig iron:* United States; 1898; unit, 1 ton (2,240 pounds).

	Amount.	Per cent of total.
Cost of labor in transforming materials	$1.18	12.29
Cost of materials and all other items except labor	8.42	87.71
Total cost	9.60	100.00

No. 320.—*Bessemer pig iron:* United States; 1897–98; unit, 1 ton (2,240 pounds).

	Amount.	Per cent of total.
Cost of labor in transforming materials	$0.80	8.00
Cost of materials and all other items except labor	9.20	92.00
Total cost	10.00	100.00

No. 351.—*Bessemer pig iron:* United States; 1897-98; unit, 1 ton (2,240 pounds).

	Amount.	Per cent of total.
Cost of labor in transforming materials	$0.60	5.88
Cost of materials and all other items except labor	9.60	94.12
Total cost	10.20	100.00

No. 352.—*Foundry pig iron:* United States; 1897; unit, 1 ton (2,240 pounds).

	Amount.	Per cent of total.
Cost of labor in transforming materials	$0.73	7.93
Cost of materials and all other items except labor	8.48	92.07
Total cost	9.21	100.00

No. 353.—*Foundry pig iron:* United States; 1897-98; unit, 1 ton (2,240 pounds).

	Amount.	Per cent of total.
Cost of labor in transforming materials	$1.00	10.26
Cost of materials and all other items except labor	8.75	89.74
Total cost	9.75	100.00

No. 354.—*Gray forge pig iron:* United States; 1898; unit, 1 ton (2,240 pounds).

	Amount.	Per cent of total.
Cost of labor in transforming materials	$0.60	6.76
Cost of materials and all other items except labor	8.27	93.24
Total cost	8.87	100.00

No. 355.—*Gray forge pig iron:* United States; 1898; unit, 1 ton (2,240 pounds).

	Amount.	Per cent of total.
Cost of labor in transforming materials	$1.28	15.26
Cost of materials and all other items except labor	7.11	84.74
Total cost	8.39	100.00

No. 356.—*Hematite pig iron:* United States; 1897; unit, 1 ton (2,240 pounds).

	Amount.	Per cent of total.
Cost of labor in transforming materials	$1.23	11.54
Cost of materials and all other items except labor	9.43	88.46
Total cost	10.66	100.00

No. 357.—*Cleveland pig iron:* Great Britain; 1897; unit, 1 ton (2,240 pounds).

	Amount.	Per cent of total.
Cost of labor in transforming materials	$0.73	7.50
Cost of materials and all other items except labor	9.00	92.50
Total cost	9.73	100.00

No. 358.—*Hematite pig iron:* Great Britain; 1897; unit, 1 ton (2,240 pounds).

	Amount.	Per cent of total.
Cost of labor in transforming materials	$0.79	6.56
Cost of materials and all other items except labor	11.25	93.44
Total cost	12.04	100.00

No. 359.—*Standard steel T rails:* United States; 1897; unit, 1 ton (2,240 pounds).

	Amount.	Per cent of total.
Cost of labor in transforming materials	$2.70	15.00
Cost of materials and all other items except labor	15.30	85.00
Total cost	18.00	100.00

No. 360.—*Light steel T rails:* United States; 1897-98; unit, 1 ton (2,240 pounds).

	Amount.	Per cent of total.
Cost of labor in transforming materials	$3.40	15.45
Cost of materials and all other items except labor	18.60	84.55
Total cost	22.00	100.00

No. 361.—*Steel rails:* Great Britain; 1890-94; unit, 1 ton, (2,240 pounds).

	Amount.	Per cent of total.
Cost of labor in transforming materials	$3.67	15.40
Cost of materials and all other items except labor	20.16	84.60
Total cost	23.83	100.00

No. 362.—*Steel rails:* Great Britain; 1897; 1 ton (2,240 pounds).
Basic Bessemer process.

	Amount.	Per cent of total.
Cost of labor in transforming materials	$1.95	10.02
Cost of materials and all other items except labor	17.52	89.98
Total cost	19.47	100.00

LEATHER.

No. 363.—*Sole leather:* United States; December, 1897; unit, 1 hide.
Oak tanned; tanned from raw hides producing an average of 42 pounds of finished leather per hide.

	Amount.	Per cent of total.
Cost of labor in transforming materials	$0.52	5.32
Cost of materials and all other items except labor	9.26	94.68
Total cost	9.78	100.00

No. 364.—*Sole leather:* United States; November, 1897; unit, 1 hide.
Oak tanned; best quality; tanned from first quality native raw hides, free from brands and without heads, producing an average of 36 pounds of finished leather per hide.

	Amount.	Per cent of total.
Cost of labor in transforming materials	$0.73	6.99
Cost of materials and all other items except labor	9.71	93.01
Total cost	10.44	100.00

No. 365.—*Sole leather:* United States; 1897; unit, 1 hide.
Oak tanned; tanned from Texas green-salted packed hides, producing an average of 47½ pounds of finished leather per hide.

	Amount.	Per cent of total.
Cost of labor in transforming materials	$0.93	10.22
Cost of materials and all other items except labor	8.17	89.78
Total cost	9.10	100.00

No. 366.—*Sole leather:* United States; 1897; unit, 1 hide.
Texas oak; tanned from raw hides, producing an average of 51.54 pounds of finished leather per hide.

	Amount.	Per cent of total.
Cost of labor in transforming materials	$0.70	7.53
Cost of materials and all other items except labor	8.60	92.47
Total cost	9.30	100.00

No. 367.—*Sole leather:* Belgium; 1897; unit, 1 hide.
Tanned from raw hide.

	Amount.	Per cent of total.
Cost of labor in transforming materials	$0.42 to $0.50	5.88 to 4.67
Cost of materials and all other items except labor	6.72 to 10.21	94.12 to 95.33
Total cost	7.14 to 10.71	100.00

No. 368.—*Sole leather:* Great Britain; 1897; unit, 1 hide.
Tanned from raw hides, producing on an average 36 pounds of leather per hide.

	Amount.	Per cent of total.
Cost of labor in transforming materials	$1.00	10.30
Cost of materials and all other items except labor	8.71	89.70
Total cost	9.71	100.00

No. 369.—*Belting leather:* United States; 1897; unit, 1 hide.
Untrimmed belting butts; tanned from native green-salted packer hides, producing an average of 40.2 pounds of untrimmed butts per hide.

	Amount.	Per cent of total.
Cost of labor in transforming materials	$0.93	9.69
Cost of materials and all other items except labor	8.67	90.31
Total cost	9.60	100.00

No. 370.—*Belting leather:* United States; April, 1898; unit, 1 hide.
Same as product No. 369, but at the different date indicated.

	Amount.	Per cent of total.
Cost of labor in transforming materials	$0.96	9.27
Cost of materials and all other items except labor	9.40	90.73
Total cost	10.36	100.00

No. 371.—*Belting leather:* Belgium; 1897; unit, 1 hide.
Tanned from raw hide.

	Amount.	Per cent of total.
Cost of labor in transforming materials	$1.00 to $1.08	11.20 to 7.56
Cost of materials and all other items except labor	7.93 to 13.20	88.80 to 92.44
Total cost	8.93 to 14.28	100.00

No. 372.—*Harness leather:* United States; 1897; unit, 1 hide.
Tanned from raw hides, producing an average of 41 pounds of finished leather per hide.

	Amount.	Per cent of total.
Cost of labor in transforming materials	$1.63	14.24
Cost of materials and all other items except labor	9.82	85.76
Total cost	11.45	100.00

No. 373.—*Harness leather:* United States; 1897–98; unit, 1 hide.
Tanned from raw hides, producing an average of 40 pounds of finished leather per hide.

	Amount.	Per cent of total.
Cost of labor in transforming materials	$1.90	18.45
Cost of materials and all other items except labor	8.40	81.55
Total cost	10.30	100.00

No. 374.—*Harness leather:* United States; 1897; unit, 1 hide.
Oak tanned from raw hides, producing an average of 37.2 pounds of finished leather per hide.

	Amount.	Per cent of total.
Cost of labor in transforming materials	$1.54	14.18
Cost of materials and all other items except labor	9.32	85.82
Total cost	10.86	100.00

No. 375.—*Harness leather:* United States; 1897; unit, 1 hide.
Oak tanned from green salted native steer hides, producing an average of 40.4 pounds of finished leather per hide.

	Amount.	Per cent of total.
Cost of labor in transforming materials	$1.29	13.35
Cost of materials and all other items except labor	8.37	86.65
Total cost	9.66	100.00

No. 376.—*Harness leather:* Belgium; 1897; unit, 1 hide.
Tanned from raw hides.

	Amount.	Per cent of total.
Cost of labor in transforming materials	$0.91 to $0.98	14.56 to 12.20
Cost of materials and all other items except labor	5.34 to 7.05	85.44 to 87.80
Total cost	6.25 to 8.03	100.00

POTTERY PRODUCTS.

No. 377.—*Ironstone china plates:* United States; 1897; unit, 1 dozen.
6-inch (actual diameter, 8 inches); plain; undecorated; weight, 12 ounces per plate.

	Amount.	Per cent of total.
Cost of labor in transforming materials	$0.1076	35.81
Cost of materials and all other items except labor	.1929	64.19
Total cost	.3005	100.00

No. 378.—*Ironstone china plates:* United States; 1897; unit, 1 dozen.
6-inch (actual diameter, 7½ inches); plain; undecorated; weight, 12 ounces per plate.

	Amount.	Per cent of total.
Cost of labor in transforming materials	$0.1460	40.00
Cost of materials and all other items except labor	.2190	60.00
Total cost	.3650	100.00

No. 379.—*Ironstone china plates:* United States; 1897; unit, 1 dozen.
7-inch (actual diameter, 9 inches); plain; undecorated; weight, 15½ ounces per plate.

	Amount.	Per cent of total.
Cost of labor in transforming materials	$0.1139	33.61
Cost of materials and all other items except labor	.2250	66.39
Total cost	.3389	100.00

No. 380.—*Ironstone china plates:* United States; 1897; unit, 1 dozen.
7-inch (actual diameter, 8½ inches); plain; undecorated; weight, 15 ounces per plate.

	Amount.	Per cent of total.
Cost of labor in transforming materials	$0.1924	45.01
Cost of materials and all other items except labor	.2351	54.99
Total cost	.4275	100.00

No. 381.—*Ironstone china plates:* United States; 1897; unit, 1 dozen.
8-inch (actual diameter, 9¾ inches); plain; undecorated; weight, 18½ ounces per plate.

	Amount.	Per cent of total.
Cost of labor in transforming materials	$0.1233	32.44
Cost of materials and all other items except labor	.2568	67.56
Total cost	.3801	100.00

No. 382.—*Ironstone china plates:* United States; 1897; unit, 1 dozen.
8-inch (actual diameter, 9⅝ inches); plain; undecorated; weight, 20 ounces per plate.

	Amount.	Per cent of total.
Cost of labor in transforming materials	$0.2208	47.41
Cost of materials and all other items except labor	.2449	52.59
Total cost	.4657	100.00

No. 383.—*Ironstone china plates:* Belgium; 1897; unit, 1 dozen.
8½-inch; plain; undecorated; ½ strength; average quality.

	Amount.	Per cent of total.
Cost of labor in transforming materials	$0.2050	32.97
Cost of materials and all other items except labor	.4168	67.03
Total cost	.6218	100.00

No. 384.—*Ironstone china plates:* Great Britain; 1897; unit, 1 dozen.
8-inch (actual diameter, 9⅝ inches); plain; undecorated; weight, 19½ ounces per plate; average quality.

	Amount.	Per cent of total.
Cost of labor in transforming materials	$0.1520	41.66
Cost of materials and all other items except labor	.2129	58.34
Total cost	.3649	100.00

No. 385.—*Ironstone china plates:* Great Britain; 1897; unit, 1 dozen.
7-inch (actual diameter, 9 inches); plain; undecorated; weight, 14 ounces per plate; average quality.

	Amount.	Per cent of total.
Cost of labor in transforming materials	$0.1014	33.33
Cost of materials and all other items except labor	.2028	66.67
Total cost	.3042	100.00

No. 386.—*Ironstone china cups and saucers:* United States; 1897; unit, 1 dozen.
Cups with handles; plain; undecorated; style, "London teas" or "large teas."

	Amount.	Per cent of total.
Cost of labor in transforming materials	$0.2295	47.24
Cost of materials and all other items except labor	.2563	52.76
Total cost	.4858	100.00

No. 387.—*Ironstone china cups and saucers:* United States; 1897; unit, 1 dozen. Of same general description as product No. 386.

	Amount.	Per cent of total.
Cost of labor in transforming materials	$0.2171	46.99
Cost of materials and all other items except labor	.2449	53.01
Total cost	.4620	100.00

No. 388.—*Ironstone china cups:* Belgium; 1897; unit, 1 dozen. With handles; plain; undecorated; average quality; capacity, 5.4 ounces.

	Amount.	Per cent of total.
Cost of labor in transforming materials	$0.1505	41.92
Cost of materials and all other items except labor	.2085	58.08
Total cost	.3590	100.00

No. 389.—*Ironstone china cups and saucers:* Great Britain; 1897; unit, 1 dozen. Cups with handles; plain; undecorated; style, "London teas" or "large teas."

	Amount.	Per cent of total.
Cost of labor in transforming materials	$0.1217	25.01
Cost of materials and all other items except labor	.3650	74.99
Total cost	.4867	100.00

WOOLEN GOODS.

No. 390.—*Blankets:* United States; 1897; unit, 1 pound. White; best grade; all wool; warp, 16 cut; filling, 10 cut; 16 threads of warp and 38 picks of filling per inch; size, 72x80 inches; weight, 6 pounds.

	Amount.	Per cent of total.
Cost of labor in transforming materials	$0.145	15.56
Cost of materials and all other items except labor	.787	84.44
Total cost	.932	100.00

No. 391.—*Blankets:* United States; 1897; unit, 1 pound. White; navy; all wool; warp, 7¼ cut; filling, 6¼ cut; 24 threads of warp and 24 picks of filling per inch; size, 58x78 inches; weight, 3¼ pounds.

	Amount.	Per cent of total.
Cost of labor in transforming materials	$0.0978	15.28
Cost of materials and all other items except labor	.5422	84.72
Total cost	.6400	100.00

No. 392.—*Blankets:* United States; 1897; unit, 1 pound. White; medium grade; all wool; same general description as product No. 390, but made of cheaper quality wool.

	Amount.	Per cent of total.
Cost of labor in transforming materials	$0.13	18.57
Cost of materials and all other items except labor	.57	81.43
Total cost	.70	100.00

No. 393.—*Blankets:* United States; 1897; unit, 1 pound.

All wool; warps, 11 cut; filling, 9 cut; $23\frac{3}{4}$ threads of warp and 27 picks of filling per inch; size, 58x76 inches; weight, 2 pounds.

	Amount.	Per cent of total.
Cost of labor in transforming materials	$0.1417	31.40
Cost of materials and all other items except labor	.3096	68.60
Total cost	.4513	100.00

No. 394.—*Blankets:* United States; 1897; unit, 1 pound.

White; best grade; cotton warp and wool filling: warp, No. 16; filling, 10 cut; 52 threads of warp and 42 picks of filling per inch; size, 60x72 inches; weight, 5 pounds.

	Amount.	Per cent of total.
Cost of labor in transforming materials	$0.125	15.76
Cost of materials and all other items except labor	.668	84.24
Total cost	.793	100.00

No. 395.—*Blankets:* United States; 1897; unit, 1 pound.

White; mixed cotton and wool; warp, 10 cut; filling, 10 cut; 36 threads of warp and 36 picks of filling per inch; size, 60x72 inches; weight, 5 pounds.

	Amount.	Per cent of total.
Cost of labor in transforming materials	$0.135	16.71
Cost of materials and all other items except labor	.673	83.29
Total cost	.808	100.00

No. 396.—*Blankets:* United States; 1897; unit, 1 pound.

Brown-gray; low grade; cotton warp and wool filling; warp, No. 10; filling, 4 cut; 24 threads of warp and 22 picks of filling per inch; size, 50x72 inches; weight, 5 pounds.

	Amount.	Per cent of total.
Cost of labor in transforming materials	$0.0825	48.13
Cost of materials and all other items except labor	.0889	51.87
Total cost	.1714	100.00

No. 397.—*Blankets:* United States; 1897; unit, 1 pound.

Blue-gray; cotton warp and wool filling; warp, No. 10; filling, 6 cut; 34 threads of warp and 32 picks of filling per inch; size, 60x72 inches; weight, 6 pounds.

	Amount.	Per cent of total.
Cost of labor in transforming materials	$0.0750	29.90
Cost of materials and all other items except labor	.1758	70.10
Total cost	.2508	100.00

No. 398.—*Blankets:* United States; 1897; unit, 1 pound.
Blue; cotton warp and wool filling; warp, No. 10; filling, 4 cut; 33½ threads of warp and 38 picks of filling per inch; size, 60x76 inches; weight, 3½ pounds.

	Amount.	Per cent of total.
Cost of labor in transforming materials	$0.0892	29.36
Cost of materials and all other items except labor	.2146	70.64
Total cost	.3038	100.00

No. 399.—*Blankets:* United States; 1897; unit, 1 pound.
Horse; best grade; all wool; warp and filling, both 5-cut; 24 threads of warp and 24 picks of filling per inch; size, 84x90 inches; weight, 7½ pounds.

	Amount.	Per cent of total.
Cost of labor in transforming materials	$0.1050	20.22
Cost of materials and all other items except labor	.4144	79.78
Total cost	.5194	100.00

No. 400.—*Blankets:* United States; 1897; unit, 1 pound.
Horse; medium grade; all wool; warp and filling, both 5-cut; 22 threads of warp and 22 picks of filling per inch; size, 84x90 inches; weight, 7 pounds.

	Amount.	Per cent of total.
Cost of labor in transforming materials	$0.0850	19.07
Cost of materials and all other items except labor	.3607	80.93
Total cost	.4457	100.00

No. 401.—*Blankets:* United States; 1897; unit, 1 pound.
Horse; plaid; all wool; warp and filling, both 4½-cut; 21½ threads of warp and 17 picks of filling per inch; size, 78x80 inches; weight, 5 pounds.

	Amount.	Per cent of total.
Cost of labor in transforming materials	$0.1000	21.42
Cost of materials and all other items except labor	.3669	78.58
Total cost	.4669	100.00

No. 402.—*Blankets:* United States; 1897; unit, 1 pound.
Horse; low grade; mixed wool and cotton; warp and filling, both 4-cut; 20 threads of warp and 20 picks of filling per inch; size, 84x90 inches; weight, 7 pounds.

	Amount.	Per cent of total.
Cost of labor in transforming materials	$0.0550	32.09
Cost of materials and all other items except labor	.1164	67.91
Total cost	.1714	100.00

No 403.—*Blankets:* United States; 1897; unit, 1 pound.
Horse; blue; cotton warp and wool filling; warp, No. 10; filling, 4-cut; 32½ threads of warp and 48 picks of filling per inch; size, 81x90 inches; weight, 7 pounds.

	Amount.	Per cent of total.
Cost of labor in transforming materials	$0.0714	24.43
Cost of materials and all other items except labor	.2209	75.57
Total cost	.2923	100.00

No. 404.—*Blankets:* Belgium; 1897; unit, 1 pound.
White; all wool; medium quality.

	Amount.	Per cent of total.
Cost of labor in transforming materials	$0.0525	14.99
Cost of materials and all other items except labor	.2977	85.01
Total cost	.3502	100.00

No. 405.—*Cloth:* United States; March, 1898; unit, 1 yard.
Beaver; 54 inches wide; weight, 29 ounces per yard; warp yarn, No. 16 colored cotton; weft yarn, ⅞ of 2¼ run and ⅛ of 1 run shoddy; 85 ends of warp and 62 picks of weft per inch.

	Amount.	Per cent of total.
Cost of labor in transforming materials	$0.240	28.20
Cost of materials and all other items except labor	.611	71.80
Total cost	.851	100.00

No. 406.—*Cloth:* United States; March, 1898; unit, 1 yard.
Cassimere; 54 inches wide; weight, 20½ ounces per yard; warp yarn, 2¼-run; weft yarn, 2⅝-run; 50 ends of warp and 36 picks of weft per inch.

	Amount.	Per cent of total.
Cost of labor in transforming materials	$0.20	23.81
Cost of materials and all other items except labor	.64	76.19
Total cost	.84	100.00

No. 407.—*Cloth:* United States; March, 1898; unit, 1 yard.
Cassimere; 54 inches wide; weight, 22 ounces per yard; warp yarn, 2-run; weft yarn, 2¾-run; 50 ends of warp and 36 picks of filling per inch.

	Amount.	Per cent of total.
Cost of labor in transforming materials	$0.2100	23.80
Cost of materials and all other items except labor	.6725	76.20
Total cost	.8825	100.00

No. 408.—*Cloth:* United States; 1897; unit, 1 yard.
Cassimere; 54 inches wide; weight, 26 ounces per yard; warp yarn, 4-run; weft yarn, 5-run; 75 ends of warp and 64 picks of weft per inch.

	Amount.	Per cent of total.
Cost of labor in transforming materials	$0.3654	28.31
Cost of materials and all other items except labor	.9252	71.69
Total cost	1.2906	100.00

No. 409.—*Cloth:* United States; 1897; unit, 1 yard.
Cassimere; 54 inches wide; weight, 20 ounces per yard; warp yarn, 4-run; weft yarn, 5-run; 60 ends of warp and 52 picks of weft per inch.

	Amount.	Per cent of total.
Cost of labor in transforming materials	$0.2801	28.09
Cost of materials and all other items except labor	.7172	71.91
Total cost	.9973	100.00

No. 410.—*Cloth:* United States; 1897; unit, 1 yard.

Cassimere; 55 inches wide; weight, 22 ounces per yard; 4½-run yarn, single, doubled, and twisted, is used in both warp and weft; 38 ends of warp and 38 picks of weft per inch.

	Amount.	Per cent of total.
Cost of labor in transforming materials	$0.2163	17.30
Cost of materials and all other items except labor	1.0337	82.70
Total cost	1.2500	100.00

No. 411.—*Cloth:* United States; November, 1897; unit, 1 yard.

Cheviot; 56 inches wide; weight, 32 ounces per yard; warp yarn, two-ply No. 24 worsted face and 2⅛-run wool; back weft yarn, 2¾-run face and 2-run back; 86 ends of warp and 60 picks of weft per inch.

	Amount.	Per cent of total.
Cost of labor in transforming materials	$0.42	28.00
Cost of materials and all other items except labor	1.08	72.00
Total cost	1.50	100.00

No. 412.—*Cloth:* United States; November, 1897; unit, 1 yard.

Cheviot; 55 inches wide; weight, 28 ounces per yard; 1¼ run yarn used in both warp and weft; 38 ends of warp and 32 picks of weft per inch.

	Amount.	Per cent of total.
Cost of labor in transforming materials	$0.22	22.45
Cost of materials and all other items except labor	.76	77.55
Total cost	.98	100.00

No. 413.—*Cloth:* United States; 1897; unit, 1 yard.

Cheviot; half shoddy; 56 inches wide; weight, 22 ounces per yard; 1⅝ run yarn is used in both warp and weft; 28 ends of warp and 26 ends of weft per inch.

	Amount.	Per cent of total.
Cost of labor in transforming materials	$0.15	28.30
Cost of materials and all other items except labor	.38	71.70
Total cost	.53	100.00

No. 414.—*Cloth:* United States; November, 1897; unit, 1 yard.

Cheviot; piece dyed; 55 inches wide; weight, 20 ounces per yard; 2 threads of 3¾ runs each, doubled and twisted, used in both warp and weft; 40 ends of warp and 30 picks of weft per inch.

	Amount.	Per cent of total.
Cost of labor in transforming materials	$0.1688	22.51
Cost of materials and all other items except labor	.5812	77.49
Total cost	.7500	100.00

No. 415.—*Cloth:* United States; 1897; unit, 1 yard.

Kersey; high grade; finely finished; 55 inches wide; weight, 20 ounces per yard; 4½ run yarn is used in both warp and weft; 48 ends of warp and 48 picks of weft per inch.

	Amount.	Per cent of total.
Cost of labor in transforming materials	$0.54	30.86
Cost of materials and all other items except labor	1.21	69.14
Total cost	1.75	100.00

No. 416.—*Cloth:* United States; November, 1897; unit, 1 yard.

Kersey; 55 inches wide; weight, 27 ounces per yard; warp yarn, 4 run; weft yarn, 4½ run face and 2 run back; 76 ends of warp and 60 picks of weft per inch.

	Amount.	Per cent of total.
Cost of labor in transforming materials	$0.38	31.93
Cost of materials and all other items except labor	.81	68.07
Total cost	1.19	100.00

No. 417.—*Cloth:* United States; November, 1897; unit, 1 yard.

Kersey; piece dyed; 55 inches wide; weight, 32 ounces per yard; warp yarn, ⅔ of 7 run and ⅓ of 2¾ run; weft yarn, ⅔ of 5 run and ⅓ of 2½ run; 88 ends of warp and 66 picks of weft per inch.

	Amount.	Per cent of total.
Cost of labor in transforming materials	$0.4202	22.47
Cost of materials and all other items except labor	1.4498	77.53
Total cost	1.8700	100.00

No. 418.—*Cloth:* United States; 1897; unit, 1 yard.

Kersey; one-third shoddy; 56 inches wide; weight, 28 ounces per yard; warp yarn, 20 ends of 3½ run and 20 ends of 1½ run per inch; weft yarn, 2 run; 40 ends of warp and 40 picks of weft per inch.

	Amount.	Per cent of total.
Cost of labor in transforming materials	$0.288	25.09
Cost of materials and all other items except labor	.860	74.91
Total cost	1.148	100.00

No. 419.—*Cloth:* United States; November, 1897; unit, 1 yard.

Kersey; half shoddy; piece dyed; 55 inches wide; weight, 32 ounces per yard; warp yarn, ⅔ of 3 run and ⅓ of 1 run; weft yarn, 2¼ run; 54 ends of warp and 40 picks of weft per inch.

	Amount.	Per cent of total.
Cost of labor in transforming materials	$0.2388	28.09
Cost of materials and all other items except labor	.6112	71.91
Total cost	.8500	100.00

No. 420.—*Cloth:* United States; November, 1897: unit, 1 yard.
Frieze; 55 inches wide; weight, 32 ounces per yard; warp yarn, 3¼ run; weft yarn, 1½ run; 41 ends of warp and 44 picks of weft per inch.

	Amount.	Per cent of total.
Cost of labor in transforming materials	$0.26	25.49
Cost of materials and all other items except labor	.76	74.51
Total cost	1.02	100.00

No. 421.—*Cloth:* United States; 1897: unit, 1 yard.
Melton; 51 inches wide; weight, 28 ounces per yard; warp yarn, 3 run; weft yarn, 3¼ run; 58 ends of warp and 54 picks of weft per inch.

	Amount.	Per cent of total.
Cost of labor in transforming materials	$0.2549	25.67
Cost of materials and all other items except labor	.7381	74.33
Total cost	.9930	100.00

No. 422.—*Cloth:* United States; November, 1897; unit, 1 yard.
Thibet; 55 inches wide; weight, 23 ounces per yard; 3½ run yarn used in both warp and weft; 95 ends of warp and 46 picks of weft per inch.

	Amount.	Per cent of total.
Cost of labor in transforming materials	$0.32	28.57
Cost of materials and all other items except labor	.80	71.43
Total cost	1.12	100.00

No. 423.—*Cloth:* United States; November, 1897; unit, 1 yard.
Thibet; piece dyed; 55 inches wide; weight, 22 ounces per yard; warp yarn, 5 run; weft yarn, 1½ run; 46 ends of warp and 32 picks of weft per inch.

	Amount.	Per cent of total.
Cost of labor in transforming materials	$0.1825	28.08
Cost of materials and all other items except labor	.4675	71.92
Total cost	.6500	100.00

No. 424.—*Cloth:* United States; November, 1897; unit, 1 yard.
Tricot; piece dyed; 32 inches wide; weight, 3¼ ounces per yard; 6½ run yarn used in both warp and weft; 35 ends of warp and 26 picks of weft per inch.

	Amount.	Per cent of total.
Cost of labor in transforming materials	$0.035	25.00
Cost of materials and all other items except labor	.105	75.00
Total cost	.140	100.00

No. 425.—*Cloth:* United States; November, 1897; unit, 1 yard.
Whip cord; 55 inches wide; weight, 22 ounces per yard; warp yarn, 5¾ run and 9 run, twisted; weft yarn, 4 run; 98 ends of warp and 40 picks of weft per inch.

	Amount.	Per cent of total.
Cost of labor in transforming materials	$0.38	24.36
Cost of materials and all other items except labor	1.18	75.64
Total cost	1.56	100.00

No. 426.—*Cloth:* United States; November, 1897; unit, 1 yard.
Woolen cloth; 55 inches wide; weight, 23 to 24 ounces per yard; warp yarn, 2-ply 3½ run wool; weft yarn, 2-ply $\frac{7}{16}$ worsted; 30 picks per inch.

	Amount.	Per cent of total.
Cost of labor in transforming materials	$0.24	16.44
Cost of materials and all other items except labor	1.22	83.56
Total cost	1.46	100.00

No. 427.—*Cloth:* Great Britain; 1897; unit, 1 yard.
Cheviot; 54 inches wide; worsted warp and woolen weft; warp 2 fold No. 10 worsted; weft No. 9½ and No. 30 twist; 20 picks per inch.

	Amount.	Per cent of total.
Cost of labor in transforming materials	$0.2233	29.45
Cost of materials and all other items except labor	.5349	70.55
Total cost	.7582	100.00

No. 428.—*Cloth:* Great Britain; 1897; unit, 1 yard.
Melton; 54 inches wide; woolen warp and weft: warp No. 12; weft No. 12; 32 picks per inch.

	Amount.	Per cent of total.
Cost of labor in transforming materials	$0.2026	29.89
Cost of materials and all other items except labor	.4752	70.11
Total cost	.6778	100.00

No. 429.—*Cloth:* Great Britain; 1897; unit, 1 yard.
Undress worsted; 56 inches wide; woolen warp and weft; warp No. 18; weft No. 18; 50 picks per inch.

	Amount.	Per cent of total.
Cost of labor in transforming materials	$0.2407	25.15
Cost of materials and all other items except labor	.7162	74.85
Total cost	.9569	100.00

No. 430.—*Woolen yarn:* United States: 1897-98; unit, 1 pound.
No. 1 yarn.

	Amount.	Per cent of total.
Cost of labor in transforming materials	$0.0260	5.44
Cost of materials and all other items except labor	.4522	94.56
Total cost	.4782	100.00

No. 431.—*Woolen yarn:* United States; December, 1897; unit, 1 pound.
No. 2 yarn.

	Amount.	Per cent of total.
Cost of labor in transforming materials	$0.0287	4.74
Cost of materials and all other items except labor	.5773	95.26
Total cost	.6060	100.00

No. 432.—*Woolen yarn:* United States; November, 1897; unit, 1 pound. No. 2 yarn.

	Amount.	Per cent of total.
Cost of labor in transforming materials	$0.0800	21.82
Cost of materials and all other items except labor	.2866	78.18
Total cost	.3666	100.00

No. 433.—*Woolen yarn:* United States; 1897-98; unit, 1 pound. No. 3 yarn.

	Amount.	Per cent of total.
Cost of labor in transforming materials	$0.0382	7.11
Cost of materials and all other items except labor	.4987	92.89
Total cost	.5369	100.00

No. 434.—*Woolen yarn:* United States; December, 1897; unit, 1 pound. No. 3 yarn.

	Amount.	Per cent of total.
Cost of labor in transforming materials	$0.0337	5.50
Cost of materials and all other items except labor	.5788	94.50
Total cost	.6125	100.00

No. 435.—*Woolen yarn:* United States; November, 1897; unit, 1 pound. No. 3½ yarn.

	Amount.	Per cent of total.
Cost of labor in transforming materials	$0.1000	23.12
Cost of materials and all other items except labor	.3325	76.88
Total cost	.4325	100.00

No. 436.—*Woolen yarn:* United States; December, 1897; unit, 1 pound. No. 4 yarn.

	Amount.	Per cent of total.
Cost of labor in transforming materials	$0.0412	6.49
Cost of materials and all other items except labor	.5938	93.51
Total cost	.6350	100.00

No. 437.—*Woolen yarn:* United States; 1897-98; unit, 1 pound. No. 5 yarn.

	Amount.	Per cent of total.
Cost of labor in transforming materials	$0.0640	10.48
Cost of materials and all other items except labor	.5469	89.52
Total cost	.6109	100.00

No. 438.—*Woolen yarn:* United States; December, 1897; unit, 1 pound. No. 5 yarn.

	Amount.	Per cent of total.
Cost of labor in transforming materials	$0.0512	7.71
Cost of materials and all other items except labor	.6133	92.29
Total cost	.6645	100.00

No. 439.—*Woolen yarn:* United States; November, 1897; unit, 1 pound. No. 5½ yarn.

	Amount.	Per cent of total.
Cost of labor in transforming materials	$0.1200	22.37
Cost of materials and all other items except labor	.4165	77.63
Total cost	.5365	100.00

No. 440.—*Woolen yarn:* United States; 1897–98; unit, 1 pound. No. 6 yarn.

	Amount.	Per cent of total.
Cost of labor in transforming materials	$0.0742	11.88
Cost of materials and all other items except labor	.5505	88.12
Total cost	.6247	100.00

No. 441.—*Woolen yarn:* United States; December, 1897; unit, 1 pound. No. 6 yarn.

	Amount.	Per cent of total.
Cost of labor in transforming materials	$0.0637	9.29
Cost of materials and all other items except labor	.6218	90.71
Total cost	.6855	100.00

No. 442.—*Woolen yarn:* United States; 1897–98; unit, 1 pound. No. 8 yarn.

	Amount.	Per cent of total.
Cost of labor in transforming materials	$0.0941	13.51
Cost of materials and all other items except labor	.6025	86.49
Total cost	.6966	100.00

No. 443.—*Woolen yarn:* United States; November, 1897; unit, 1 pound. No. 9 yarn.

	Amount.	Per cent of total.
Cost of labor in transforming materials	$0.1500	19.85
Cost of materials and all other items except labor	.6055	80.15
Total cost	.7555	100.00

No. 444.—*Woolen yarn:* United States; 1897–98; unit, 1 pound. No. 10 yarn.

	Amount.	Per cent of total.
Cost of labor in transforming materials	$0.1085	14.65
Cost of materials and all other items except labor	.6322	85.35
Total cost	.7407	100.00

No. 445.—*Woolen yarn:* Belgium; 1897; unit, 1 pound.

	Amount.	Per cent of total.
Cost of labor in transforming materials	$0.0700	26.66
Cost of materials and all other items except labor	.1926	73.34
Total cost	.2626	100.00

No. 446.—*Woolen yarn:* Belgium; 1897; unit, 1 pound.

	Amount.	Per cent of total.
Cost of labor in transforming materials	$0.0306	11.65
Cost of materials and all other items except labor	.2320	88.35
Total cost	.2626	100.00

O

www.ingramcontent.com/pod-product-compliance
Lightning Source LLC
Chambersburg PA
CBHW020307090426
42735CB00009B/1250

* 9 7 8 3 3 3 7 1 5 4 2 5 7 *